"*Armed: Principles for Developing an Intercessory Prayer Team* is both inspiring and practical. Biblically well thought out, it provides much needed practical guidelines for intercessory prayer, as well as structure for developing prayer teams. Eric tackles the important task of establishing a healthy culture complete with protocols. This book is a must for churches wanting to establish an intercessory ministry as well as for the individual who wants to learn more about intercession."

Dr. Tom Jones
Executive Vice President and CFO of Global Awakening
Dean of Global Awakening Theological Seminary (GATS)
Director of the Apostolic Network of Global Awakening

"Eric has a constant heart for ministry and building others up through equipping the saints and serving the Church. Although Eric is gifted in many areas of ministry it doesn't surprise me that this book's emphasis is on prayer. I believe the Holy Spirit is bringing the believer and the Church back to the power of prayer so we can bring heaven to earth as Jesus taught us to pray. This book, *Armed*, brings the believer into understanding the power of prayer and how to walk in it on many different levels. Eric's style of writing will make it hard for you to put this book down as his stories and examples are backed by biblical texts. I recommend that you read this book as a training manual for your prayer life."

Paul Martini
Lead Pastor, New Life City, Albuquerque, NM

"I have had the pleasure of ministering alongside Eric over the last 14 years and can vouch for the effectiveness of the principles he shares to develop an intercessory prayer team. As a church, we have benefitted greatly from Eric's understanding of intercessory prayer and its biblical application, and it is my prayer that your church or ministry would also benefit as you apply what you learn from reading *Armed*. We are all called to pray, but read this book and you'll be arming yourself with the tools necessary for the privilege of going into battle as an intercessor. *Armed* is practical, informative, and full of great ideas for the leader wanting to grow or establish an intercessory prayer team."

John Robertson
Senior Pastor, Riverlife Baptist Church

"In his book *Armed*, Eric Whitley provides spiritually powerful practical insights and godly wisdom for the development and training of intercessory prayer teams. From many years of experience, he highlights life changing examples and testimonies of the effectiveness of prayer. You will be convinced of the necessity of the ministry of intercessory prayer for your church or ministry, and Eric will show you how it can be done."

Dr Tom Litteer
Professor of Hermeneutics and Assistant Dean
Global Awakening Theological Seminary

"Eric Whitley brings practical wisdom and principles for intercessory prayer formed by over a decade of experience as a church leader in his book *Armed*. Be guided through the wild lands of intercessory prayer and discover the rich rewards of this battle. A book like this must be lived and tested before it can be written for our benefit."

Ryan Vallee
Church Engagement, Alpha Australia

"From cover to cover, *Armed* is a Holy Spirit inspired book for every intercessor and those leading a team. Whether you are just starting out or a seasoned church leader, this book will clearly help you navigate every aspect of forming and leading an intercessory prayer team. It is filled with tried and tested life experiences of a proven leader in the area of prayer. This book will arm every intercessor, pastor, or ministry leader to understand and apply their kingdom power and authority to find spiritual solutions to the challenges their church faces."

Rob Spurr
Global Director Prophetic Finders, Member of the Australia and Queensland Prophetic Council

"Prayer is certainly one of the most important gifts from our Father. It is our direct and intimate connection, allowing us to praise Him, appeal to Him, and intercede to Him on behalf of others. In this wonderful book, Eric clearly and succinctly gives us guidelines and methods to improve how we pray. He also gives us insights on how to build teams of intercessors and manage those teams. But it's not only a book for a church intercessory team; these principles can most definitely be used for the individual who wants a powerful and rewarding prayer life. Eric's years of experience in prayer ministry and intimacy with God is clearly evident as he shares his knowledge with us. What a blessing!"

Rodney Callanan
Co-founder & Director, Droplets In A Stream

ARMED

PRINCIPLES FOR DEVELOPING AN INTERCESSORY PRAYER TEAM

ERIC M. WHITLEY

KINGFISHER

Copyright © 2022 by Eric M. Whitley

All rights reserved.

No part of this book may be reproduced in any form or by any electronic or mechanical means, including information storage and retrieval systems, without written permission from the author, except for the use of brief quotations in a book review.

All Scripture quotations, unless otherwise noted, are taken from the *Holy Bible, New International Version® NIV ®*. Copyright © 1973, 1978, 1984 by International Bible Society. Used by permission of Zondervan. All rights reserved.

Scripture quotations marked TPT are from The Passion Translation®. Copyright © 2017, 2018, 2020 by Passion & Fire Ministries, Inc. Used by permission. All rights reserved. ThePassionTranslation.com.

Scripture quotations identified NKJV are from the New King James Version®. Copyright © 1982 by Thomas Nelson, Inc. Used by permission. All rights reserved.

Published by Kingfisher Press, an imprint of Kingfisher Ministries.

Cover design by Erin D'Ameron Hill

This book is dedicated to my wife, Bronwen. Without your love, support, and encouragement over many years, this book would not be possible.

CONTENTS

Introduction	xiii
1. The Principle of Unity	1
2. The Displacement Principle	21
3. Understanding the Principles of Spiritual Authority Part 1	35
4. Understanding the Principles of Spiritual Authority Part 2	55
5. The Principles of Faith and Fear	69
6. The Principles of Contending Prayer and Fasting	91
7. Prophetic Symbolism in Intercession	117
8. Utilizing Spiritual Gifts within a Team	131
9. Practical Matters	155
10. Succession Planning	183
11. Final Thoughts	207
Afterword	211
About the Author	213

INTRODUCTION

Prayer is one of the most fundamental activities of the Christian life. When we pray, whether it is for ourselves or others, we are conversing with God to gain His insight for the situations we are facing. When we pray, we are seeking answers, communion with our Father, and power for our lives. Prayer is powerful. It changes us, changes our perspective, and changes the world.

Unfortunately, most of us take prayer for granted and use it as a last resort when we feel out of our depth or at the end of our rope. Prayer is not meant to be a Christian's problem-solving machine; it is meant to connect us to God in a way that transforms our earthly perspectives to align with God's divine perspective. This is the work of an intercessor.

Intercessors listen to God, agree with His will, and release His power in the world through the act of praying. Intercession is a specific kind of praying that should be focused and purposeful. It should be conducted with a servant's heart motivated by love. It is often done as part of a group, but it can also be done alone. Intercession is often a way for a believer to serve his or her church and the greater community by cooperating with God's will through prayer. A group of intercessors is like a platoon in God's army that battles the forces of darkness to push them back and extend God's kingdom. Every church should have an intercessory prayer team. I have seen firsthand the power of intercession to change earthly challenges into heavenly victories. This book will hopefully help you develop an intercessory prayer team to support and serve the ministries of your church. My desire is to see the power of God released in your life, your church, and your community.

It is not difficult to find a book on prayer or intercession whether you are browsing the aisles of your favorite bookstore or scrolling on your computer or phone. This begs the question, "Why have I written a book on intercession, and why should you choose to read it?" Although you are not obligated to read it because you are one of my friends or family, I am eager to share what I have learned with you about the power of prayer from the various situations God has placed me in throughout my life and ministry. I believe I have something valuable and unique to add to the conversation.

I also want to see the Church once again become a place

of power and relevance in the world. Intercession is a powerful tool when wielded by passionate, dedicated believers to bring God's will to fruition. There are many other authors and teachers who have addressed intercession. I am indebted to them for what I have learned. Yet having gone through the challenge of developing and leading an intercessory prayer team from scratch, I feel I have discovered specific and unique aspects of intercession that I believe will help prepare you and empower you as intercessors in effective and essential ways.

Prayer is a spiritual activity, and intercession is a spiritual resource God has given to us to address earthly issues that have a spiritual origin. Intercessors serve their church community by partnering with God's will through prayer. As a spiritual entity, the church faces challenges and problems that need to be addressed spiritually because worldly solutions are often inadequate. Therefore, prayer is the spiritual strategy that must be employed before we try to use earthly reason, programming, or planning to address the obstacles we face in the church. I have seen prayer set the demonized free, heal terminal illness, shift dark atmospheres, and bring peace in the most difficult circumstances. I have seen and experienced some incredible things during my life that have all occurred through the activity of prayer. God has used many weird and wonderful moments for a purpose, even though I have not always seen it that way. I hope that my experiences, mistakes, and the gems of wisdom I have garnered over more than twenty years of pastoral ministry will bless you and give you a head start beyond what I had when I first attempted to form an intercessory prayer team.

This book is for pastors and volunteer ministry leaders. My desire is to equip you with the information you need to develop an intercessory prayer team within your church. This book is also for individuals who want to learn about intercession so you may serve your church with excellence. I know the difficulties and obstacles church leaders face when developing and leading a ministry team. I have made many mistakes, but I have also seen God use ordinary believers like me to accomplish tremendous things for His kingdom. You do not have to be a Christian superhero to serve God in a powerful way. However, you do need to know how to bring people together to serve with a unified purpose. The principles I share in this book are tried and tested. I believe they will give every intercessory prayer team leader a sure foundation to build a dynamic and effective team.

About Me

Some might describe my life as a blessed accident. I am the youngest of four children by a large margin. Although my parents would never admit it, I am fairly sure my conception was a surprise! My oldest brother and sister have children who are about my age. Most of my friends at school thought my parents were my grandparents, as they were so much older. My parents married at eighteen years old and had my brother the following year. Fast forward twenty-one years, and I was born. This set up a unique family dynamic. I had three siblings, but I was essentially raised as an only child because by the time I was eight years old, my closest sibling had married and moved out of the house. It was an unusual situation, especially in the 1970s.

My parents loved me and raised me in a Christian home. My parents' example of faith taught me the value of prayer in my own life. I am very thankful for the ways they modeled their dependence on God through prayer. When faced with difficulties such as financial hardship and physical disability, it was prayer that sustained us by God's gracious and loving provision.

I grew up in one of the suburbs that surround the sprawling city of Atlanta, Georgia. I gave my life to Jesus at the age of five and was baptized at age eight. My entire life has centered around attending church. I have always loved being involved in every ministry and service that my churches have offered. I would spend multiple nights a week participating in various ministries throughout my childhood and teen years. I would sing in choirs, participate in evangelism outreaches, travel to foreign countries on mission trips, and faithfully go to Sunday school and Sunday worship every week. I went to every church camp and youth event I could. I was one of those children who wanted to be there and was never forced to go. I am so thankful that my earliest foundations of faith were cemented in the church. It was my happy place, and my relationship with God was firmly established there. God's presence and protection in my life have never wavered in over forty years.

Growing up with older parents did not particularly hinder me in my development into adulthood, but there were many challenges that I faced at an immature age that my peers were spared from until they were older. I spent a lot of time alone, and often talked to God because I did not have anyone else to talk to. When I was around the age of eleven, my father became quite ill. He developed heart disease and had many complications associated with it. Eventually, he had to stop working because he was not physically able to exert himself. His health continued to decline until he was left with only twenty percent of his heart functioning. Simple actions such as going up or down stairs left him exhausted and panting for air. If he were to live longer than a few years, he would require a heart transplant. At this point, he was only in his early fifties. My father's disability forced my mother to return to work after being a stay-at-home mom for most of her life. My world was disrupted and turned upside down. My loneliness only increased as my homelife transitioned from a stable, familiar place to a new reality of increasing independence and self-reliance. Nothing remained the same. As I entered my teens, I had to mature much quicker than my peers to help our home function.

It was prayer that sustained me during these years. I

would often fall asleep praying each night in bed. God was always good to us, and we never missed a bill or were left begging despite the minimal income my mother made working at Walmart. Those were difficult times, but God always sustained us. My mother's work schedule and my father's illness often left me feeling vulnerable and alone. I was bullied at school and had few friends. These experiences made it easy for fear to assault my life.

Fear attacked me through multiple supernatural experiences. The enemy is a coward and always tries to exploit our weak areas. As a young person, I did not have the maturity to know how to respond to these attacks in a way that did not leave me feeling fearful and powerless. The demonic world seemed so much more powerful than anything else I had known. Looking back, I can now see how God used those experiences to build a resilience in me that I would need as a pastor many years later.

One of the most significant experiences I had as a child was visiting my oldest brother at his home. He purchased a 150-year-old property with a house and multiple barns. It was a large, imposing home that looked like it would be a perfect location to film a horror movie. There were even Native American burial grounds on the property. It was commonly known in the community that this property was haunted. Very strange and spooky things happen in and around this house even today. Whenever we would visit, I would always have a supernatural experience that left me fearful.

Let me clarify—I do not believe in ghosts or haunted houses in the sense that most people understand them. I believe hauntings are the activity of the demonic. Although some ghosts appear to be deceased people from the past, I believe they are simply demonic spirits appearing in this way to perpetuate fear and curiosity. We must remember, demonic spirits are eternal. They existed when the deceased person lived many years earlier and would know what they looked like, how they died, and any other detail that would help them "haunt" a house.

Some of the experiences I had at this property included seeing dark figures, hearing an organ playing when it was in a distant closed-off room, hearing my name called, and hearing unexplained footsteps, bumps, and noises. There were many spooky hours spent there. I know of many other stories, and quite a few other people have had supernatural experiences at this house. I believe I experienced many of these things because the enemy was trying to create fear within me that would prevent me from stepping into my future spiritual gifts and calling.

In addition to my experiences at this house, I also had frequent demonic dreams as a child. Many were similar to the dreams some of my future clients would describe to me when I ministered inner healing as a pastor. Again, I believe the enemy was attacking me to make me afraid of the supernatural and prevent me from becoming the spiritual warrior I am today, and he succeeded for many years. I have since learned how to deal with the demonic through prayer. For those of you who have had similar experiences and still feel fearful, I hope that this book will help you see that you do have the power and authority of Jesus to overcome whatever darkness comes against you.

If you are someone who struggles with fear, you do not have to continue living this way. Jesus won the victory over all darkness on the cross. As one of His children, you can trust Him to protect and empower you to see through the lies of the enemy and defeat him with the truth.

Before you delve into the main content of this book, you might want to pray a prayer similar to the one below:

Dear Jesus,

I know You are greater than any darkness in the world. I trust You to protect my mind and heart as I read this book. Please fill me with Your love so that fear will not find a foothold in my thinking. Please hide me under Your wings as I read and teach me to stand in the authority You have given me to resist the enemy and send him fleeing.

In Jesus' name, amen.

My Call to Ministry

I felt the call to be a pastor at the age of fifteen. At that time, I thought I would be a worship pastor because music was a major part of my life. I have served as a worship pastor at several churches through the years, but it has been in the last fifteen years that God has broadened my scope of ministry and taught me how to humbly serve a congregation in a pastoral capacity. Prayer and intercession have been the key elements of my ministry. Without the power of prayer, I would never have been able to pastor the many people God brought into my life and ministry. Spiritual problems can only be solved with spiritual answers. Prayer and intercession release the power of God into our lives, removing our problems and replacing them with His blessings.

Around 2004, I was serving at a church in a rural part of Atlanta. It was an independent church plant, and the resources were lean. We only had two staff—the senior pastor and me. A young couple began attending the church and became Christians. As they continued to grow in their faith, it became obvious that the wife needed deliverance ministry. The closer she and her husband came to God, the more overt her manifestations became. You must understand that this was a Southern Baptist church (a cessationist denomination), and we were not well equipped to deal with overt supernatural matters.

One night, the senior pastor received a frantic call from

the husband because his wife was involuntarily levitating above their bed. We had to help this family, but neither the senior pastor nor I had ever confronted a demon directly or tried to minister deliverance. We planned to fast for a week and then visit this couple to pray with them to see if we could cast out the demon. This made me incredibly nervous. All my experiences with the demonic through dreams and at the haunted house were extremely negative and scary, and now I was about to directly confront what I feared most. At the time, I did not realize or understand that I have authority over the enemy. I felt extremely inadequate to minister deliverance.

We arrived at this couple's home around 7 p.m. a week later. None of us were sure what to expect. We all poured a cup of coffee and settled into the living room. The senior pastor had found some prayers and inner healing material on the internet, and we began by praying the opening prayer from this material. We never finished that prayer. The demon immediately manifested, and the lady began screaming and fell off the couch onto the floor. I remember staring in stunned silence for several minutes as her screaming and writhing continued to escalate.

Eventually, I found my presence of mind and began praying and quoting scripture. None of this made any impact. Thankfully, the senior pastor took the lead and did not flinch. Multiple times, the lady would reach for something to throw at him, but she could not muster the strength to do it as he commanded her to drop the object. This was the first time I heard tongues—not the beautiful, spiritual prayer language most are familiar with, but a demonic tongue, and the demon was not saying kind things, though I could not understand it. The chaos of the night continued for many hours until we got to a point where the lady was lucid enough to say a prayer of forgiveness for a man who had sexually assaulted her. The demon immediately left when she finished this prayer. I learned a valuable lesson that evening: God's authority enforced through prayer is powerful.

The next day, I felt quite shell-shocked and exhausted. I had never experienced anything like that before. I prayed, "God, I never want to do that again, but if You bring someone in need to me, I will minister to them." Although I did not know it at the time, that was a significant prayer that God heard and would take me up on. I believe that post-deliverance prayer was the start of my journey into inner healing, deliverance, intercession, and the prophetic.

It was several years before I faced another demon again. My wife and I had moved to Australia, where I began serving at a local church in Brisbane as their young adult pastor. Slowly, but steadily, God began bringing person after person through my door in need of deliverance. As I desperately tried to help each one, I realized that I needed to grow in this area quickly. I began reading every book I could find on deliverance. I would try to apply what I learned. I found some methodologies useful and others less effective, but I grew significantly in my understanding of the spiritual realm through this time.

One of the best things I learned was to listen to the Holy Spirit's leading and to follow His direction. No one had taught me how to receive and apply the words of knowledge I was receiving; it was all gained through trial and error. I did not even know what a word of knowledge was, or that I was operating in prophetic revelation for several years.

Paralleling my personal journey was the journey my church was taking. I was serving at a traditionally conservative Baptist church in Brisbane. After reading Dr. Randy Clark's book *There Is More*, our executive pastor decided to attend a conference Dr. Clark was conducting in Australia. His experience at the conference changed him dramatically, and that change spilled over into our church as we began to explore how to embrace the fullness of the Holy Spirit more deeply. This was a challenging time, as concepts of divine healing, prophecy, and living supernaturally were being introduced to a traditionally conservative church. I embraced these things cautiously but could not deny what God was doing. I wanted to experience God's power in my own life.

Over the next ten years, our church transitioned from a traditional Baptist church into a charismatic church that regularly sees God move in supernatural ways. We are still conservative theologically, but our expressions and practice are charismatic. This transition opened a new door for me as a pastor. I left my role as young adult pastor and became the LifeCentre pastor.

The LifeCentre was a new ministry initiative begun in 2013 that offered prayer for inner healing, deliverance, physical healing, and intercession. As part of that ministry, it was my responsibility to develop a culture of prayer for our church. I was still learning and growing in my ability to listen to God and respond appropriately. It seemed like every day was an exciting adventure as this new ministry developed. In my new role, I knew I needed to undertake some formal training, so I enrolled in Global Awakening's Christian Healing Certification Program (CHCP). I was one of their first students. I learned how to pray for physical, emotional, and spiritual healing through this program, which is firmly based on biblical practice and theology. These courses also equipped me to train others in these areas. These were exciting times in my ministry as teams developed and learned to pray for the needs of our congregation and the broader community. God was faithful, and we saw many people healed of such things as infertility, depression, cancer, and demonic oppression. It seemed like I would witness and experience something new of God's power and authority every week.

It was during this time that I began to develop intercessory prayer for our church. Once again, God took me on a journey of discovery and growth. In the beginning, I made many mistakes, but God's faithfulness and grace covered my shortcomings as the team developed. My experience developing and leading the intercessors is the foundation of this book. It is my desire that the principles and practicalities we established at my church will expedite the development of intercessory prayer at your church. I am not saying that my way is best, but it is effective and proven. If you follow these principles and practical steps, you can build a healthy and effective intercessory prayer team.

Although this book is written with a focus on pastors or ministry leaders who desire to develop or improve an intercessory prayer team, I pray that it will encourage and motivate the average reader as well. Intercession is the fireplace that warms and sustains a church. Though the ministry is often done out of the sight of the greater church, the impact is significant. Intercession is not done on a stage under bright lights, but I believe it is just as important as anything that occurs during a Sunday morning service. I hope that you will not read this book and then just put it on a shelf. My prayer is that this book becomes a resource that produces spiritual fruit in your church and community. Prayer is our most powerful weapon as a Christian. Intercession is a God-given tool of cultural change that we are to use. Please take hold of this tool and use it. It is past time for the Church to become the primary cultural leader it once was.

1

THE PRINCIPLE OF UNITY

How good and pleasant it is when God's people live together in unity! It is like precious oil poured on the head, running down on the beard, running down on Aaron's beard, down on the collar of his robe. It is as if the dew of Hermon were falling on Mount Zion. For there the Lord bestows his blessing, even life forevermore.

— PSALM 133

IN 2013, I BEGAN A NEW PASTORAL ROLE IN MY CHURCH. ONE OF my new responsibilities was to develop a culture of prayer. As such, I focused on developing an intercessory prayer team.

The only problem was that I was completely inexperienced leading a group of intercessors. When I began, I struggled to explain how intercessory prayer differed from other types of prayer. Admittedly, my impression of intercessors was a bit negative. I thought they were generally older, quirky Christians who had nothing better to do than pray for hours about a particular topic.

Before being given this new role, I had never prayed for more than a few minutes at a time. I was a typical busy pastor trying to keep my ministries running while juggling family responsibilities. The idea that I could pray for hours at a time about a singular topic seemed impossibly daunting and perhaps a bit boring. I felt insecure about leading a group of intercessors when I had never been an intercessor myself. Little did I know that God was about to expose me to some of the most wonderful experiences of my life.

My church had a fantastic discipleship program at the time, and as part of the Sunday night sessions, there was a small team of intercessors who would pray for the leaders and participants of the program. I inherited this team and tried to bring some structure to what they were doing. This did not go smoothly. As is common in most churches, the people were resistant to change, at least initially. The team was small and had been functioning for a couple of years independently without any relevant accountability or input. They did not have a recognized leader and were not looking for one. What I had hoped would be an environment to learn about intercession quickly became a battleground. Opposing sides were formed between me and those who thought they should be leading the group. I started to anxiously dread the time we met each Sunday evening.

My arrival as team leader was met with some enthusiasm, but that quickly faded when I started to implement structure and focus into what we were doing. This was my first time participating in intercession as well as leading a group, so I did not always give the best direction. It was a challenge, and I made a lot of mistakes. Due to my lack of experience, I did not know what I was doing and had to learn on the job. My intentions were sincere, but my application was flawed. Still, God was always faithful and worked through us despite our insufficiencies. Each week, we prayed for the participants and leaders going through the discipleship program, and God moved in their lives. I would not say that we took significant ground for God's kingdom that year, but God was incredibly gracious and filled in the gaps that we left because of our inadequacies.

One of the biggest challenges I faced was bringing unity to the group. We did not have a mutually agreed-upon goal for why and what we were interceding for. My insecurities as a leader only made matters worse. I made the mistake of giving the team too much say in how we functioned week to week, which created a power struggle between me and the more outspoken members of the team. They became resentful that I had been placed in leadership when they felt they had been doing fine on their own. I quickly learned that there must be a recognized leader if the team is to move forward in a unified way. We needed to learn how to cooperate with one another with mutual respect and honor.

Due to our internal team conflicts, we did not support the ministry very well that first year. The tension in the room was palpable each Sunday night. There was truly little unity within the team. As the year progressed, the group became smaller and smaller as those who did not want to follow my leadership left the team. I was frustrated and upset that I was not doing my job well. Some of the team even left the church. This left me feeling like a failure, but I did not give up. I knew I had to learn from my mistakes and do it quickly if we were ever to have an impact. I knew my leadership must improve and the team had to become more unified. Although it was incredibly uncomfortable for me personally, God was growing my ability and confidence to lead an intercessory prayer team. I learned the value of team unity and the consequences of disunity.

My first experience leading intercessors was fraught with difficulties, but God revealed a valuable principle for intercession that I have implemented ever since. I discovered that unity must be the foundation that an intercessory prayer team is built upon. There must be unity at every level of the team and the ministry it is supporting. Each team member must be unified with the others while operating toward a common agenda. Team unity must be set by strong, committed leadership that demonstrates love and compassion. The leader must be unified with the team and the team with the leader. Without unity, your effectiveness and power as an intercessory prayer team is limited significantly. If your group is not unified, you may spend more time resolving conflicts than praying.

Unity, under the best circumstances, is often difficult to cultivate. Couple that with individuals who can sometimes seem quirky, strange, or stubborn, and you have a significant challenge to address. God often calls intercessors from the fringes. They may be people who have been overlooked in other areas of ministry because they often perceive the world around them through a spiritual lens. Some might even say that intercessors are weird, but weird is often fun! Directing and unifying such unique personalities requires strong leadership, wise decision-making, and a focused eye to what the Holy Spirit is doing. Any sports team can attest to the effectiveness of a team mentality where every individual knows his or her role and executes it for the greater good. Unity is a powerful and essential dynamic when operating in the spiritual realm. By its nature, intercession is a spiritual activity.

Team unity is not just a practical principle, but a spiritual one as well. Unity is a core value of the kingdom of God.

Hebrews 12:14 encourages unity within the body of Christ. *"Make every effort to live in peace with everyone and to be holy; without holiness no one will see the Lord."* Disunity does not please God and will prevent us from operating in holiness. How can we serve those we are interceding for with attitudes of jealousy, offense, and anger in our hearts? An environment of unity ignites God's power to impact an individual, group, or ministry through intercession. Unity brings us together to work toward a common goal while cultivating a sense of belonging to something bigger than ourselves. We are always better together than on our own.

I believe team unity is so important that I have made it my first principle for developing intercessory prayer teams. One Bible passage that emphasizes the principle of unity is Matthew 18:19-20. *"Again, truly I tell you that if two of you on earth agree about anything they ask for, it will be done for them by my Father in heaven. For where two or three gather in my name, there am I with them."* What a great promise! As we come into agreement with one another in the presence of Jesus, our prayers are heard and answered. It all begins by being willing to agree with one another as we pray. Our prayers are empowered when we are unified and committed to the same purpose. If we come with multiple agendas or with offense in our heart, it becomes difficult to agree with those we are serving beside.

Disunity also limits our ability to sense God's presence with us. It is as if a spiritual veil is placed over us, making it difficult to perceive what God is saying and doing. When we become unified in the name of Jesus, He joins us as we pray. Matthew 18 says that Jesus will be with us, and His presence is powerful. I would much rather face the enemy with Jesus by my side than to confront the enemy alone.

Gather in His Name

There are several things that must be understood about Matthew 18, as it can be taken too simply and the importance of what is being said can be missed. First, we must gather in His name. If the starting point of why we meet is not unified, how are we to be effective as intercessors? We must meet with the common purpose of gathering in His name. That is a funny phrase, though. What does it mean to gather in His name? It means we acknowledge the authority of Jesus, who He is, and operate in obedience to His Word. Apart from Jesus, we can do very little to disrupt the powers of darkness in the world. Jesus has been given all authority in heaven and earth. He will stand with us during our times of intercession when we are unified. He is God's Son who sits at God's right hand. He is the Lamb Who was slain for our sins out of love for humanity and in obedience to God's purposes. To gather in His name means that we understand who He is and who we are. We have a position and a role within God's family. We are serving as intercessors in response to the relationship we have with the Father through Jesus. We are serving Jesus as well as those we are praying for when we come together to intercede.

Pray in Agreement

The next step is to agree about what we are praying for. If two or more Christians pray in agreement, it stirs the Father's heart, and He will answer. This is especially true when we align our prayers to His will and Word (1 John 5:14-15). I will expound on that later. When we meet to intercede as a team, we must pray in agreement with one another. If we are listening to another intercessor praying and our thoughts and heart disagree, it negates the power of a unified prayer. There have been times when I have witnessed two intercessors contradict one another with their prayers in a sort of spiritual one-upmanship. They were not unified, and it completely distracted the team from the purpose of our intercession.

Resolving Conflict within the Church

As I mentioned earlier, we must understand Matthew 18 properly if we are to apply it to intercession. There is more to take away from this passage than praying in agreement and gathering in His name. The author of Matthew wants the church to be unified. On their own, verses nineteen and twenty can be applied to general prayer and intercession, but the context of Matthew 18 is primarily about how to handle disagreements, conflicts, sin, and offense. All these things rob us of unity. Conflicts and disunity put a wedge between believers and God. All Christians would do well to follow the steps of Matthew 18:15-20 to resolve offense when it occurs. Our churches would be much healthier and effective if we were to do so.

If your brother or sister sins, go and point out their fault, just between the two of you. If they listen to you, you have won them over. But if they will not listen, take one or two others along, so that "every matter may be established by the testimony of two or three witnesses." If they still refuse to listen, tell it to the church; and if they refuse to listen even to the church, treat them as you would a pagan or a tax collector. Truly I tell you, whatever you bind on earth will be bound in heaven, and whatever you loose on earth will be loosed in heaven. Again, truly I tell you that if two of you on earth agree about anything they ask for, it will be done for them by my Father in heaven. For where two or three gather in my name, there am I with them.

— MATTHEW 18:15-20

Starting with verse fifteen, the author of Matthew lays out the progression that believers should follow to resolve conflicts within the church. It begins with a private, one-on-one conversation. If the offender will not listen, then you should return, again privately, with one or two other witnesses (vs. 16). We bring witnesses as this was the requirement of the Hebrew law set out in Deuteronomy 19:15. *"One witness is not enough to convict anyone accused of any crime or offense they may have committed. A matter must be established by the testimony of two or three witnesses."* If the offender continues to be unrepentant, then the matter can be brought before the church (vs. 17). Verse eighteen then explains that the decision made by the church will be bound or loosed in heaven as it is on earth. In other words, the verdict will be recognized by God because of the agreement of the church over the matter.

This is the biblical template for how to restore unity to the body when divisions arise. In the proper context, verses nineteen and twenty are the endcap to that process, assuring the church that the decisions that are made are applied in the spiritual realm as well as on earth. This means that the offender will lose fellowship within the church community until he or she decides to repent and resolve the disunity they have caused. They do not lose their salvation, but they are put out of the community of believers. They lose their intimacy of relationship with the church body. The ramifications of disunity impact our earthly relationships as well as our relationship with God. Unconfessed sin or an unwillingness to forgive may leave us with a sense of being distanced from God. Disunity among believers is a serious issue. Thankfully, there is hope of restoration in this passage. An offender will be fully restored to unity with the church and God if they do repent and turn away from their sin. Until then, they experience a separation that should lead them to a recognition of their brokenness and hopefully restoration (Ps. 51:17).

If general unity within the church is so important that there is a template given to resolve issues, then it is even more important that we intercede in a spirit of unity. The work of an intercessor is powerful and vitally important to the ministry health of a church. I believe Matthew 18 is included in the gospels because God knew that disagreements and offense would occur. If left unresolved, offenses can be devastating to the individuals involved as well as the greater church community. I am sure that all of us can think of a situation in which someone had a disagreement and left the church, leaving a trail of collateral damage behind them. As intercessors, we must be mature believers, capable of resolving conflict in a godly manner. The responsibilities of an intercessor do not leave room for jealousy, unforgiveness, and disunity to linger if we are to serve our church in an effective manner. If we hold on to such petty things, we are being disobedient to God, and we are limiting our ability to make an impact for the kingdom.

When we meet with the purpose to intercede on behalf of an individual, group, or organization, we must come with the same unified agenda. This may be the resolution of a problem or an answer to a question. You may be seeking physical healing or a blessing. You may be praying for protection or divine intervention in a circumstance. Intercession operates in the supernatural power of God. It is a spiritual activity. We do not want to limit access to God's power because we are carrying sin in our heart. We are responsible to keep short accounts with God personally. Offense will occur. How we respond to offense demonstrates our maturity or immaturity as a Christian. Offense should be dealt with quickly so we may serve in holiness (Heb. 12:14). When we gather to pray, each intercessor must be aligned with the rest of the team in their spirit and mind. When we engage in intercession as a unified team, our service becomes a powerful tool that impacts both the spiritual and earthly realms.

Unity Starts in the Heart

Unity is a heart issue. It originates within a person's beliefs and thoughts and requires a willingness to be humble and submissive. Mature intercessors should have a selfless disposition, putting others before themselves (Phil. 2:1-4). Intercession operates in humility and is motivated by love. The heart of an intercessor should beat in rhythm with the others on the team and in unison with the ministries of their church. Serving the church community is an intercessor's main priority. Pride and arrogance can easily cause disunity among a team. *"Where there is strife, there is pride, but wisdom is found in those who take advice"* (Prov. 13:10). If we think we know better or have the direct line to heaven that others do not possess, the focus can quickly move from unity to trying to direct the show. The focus becomes inward instead of heavenward. A disunified intercession session can quickly become disjointed, lose focus, and eventually bounce all over the place, firing "prayer bullets" in every direction hoping to hit the target. Intercession should be precise like a sniper rifle, not taking a machine-gun approach.

Unity requires each member of the team to honor, respect, and love the people they are serving. This is not just a requirement of an intercessor, but as Christians, we are called to love one another and to forgive when we have been offended or hurt by another believer. This is not easy, but God will bless our obedience.

Therefore, as God's chosen people, holy and dearly loved, clothe yourselves with compassion, kindness, humility, gentleness, and patience. Bear with each other and forgive one another if any of you has a grievance against someone. Forgive as the Lord forgave you. And over all these

> *virtues put on love, which binds them all together in perfect unity.*
>
> — COLOSSIANS 3:12-14

Love must be the underlying factor that unifies us, love for God and love for each other. A mature intercessor puts on the cloak of God's love to remain in perfect unity. God's love gives us a common point to start from. We must love the people we are serving and those we serve alongside.

There are four relationships that require unity as intercessors. We must be unified with our team leaders, fellow team members, church leadership, and God. Each relationship requires humility and submission. If there is offense or disunity within these relationships, we may be giving the enemy authority to hinder our prayers. We must examine our hearts with the help of the Holy Spirit to see if we are holding any offense or rebellion toward those we are serving.

Unified with Leadership

Following the team leader's lead is important. This may not always be easy, as we all have an opinion about how things should go. We must trust our team leader and support their direction. Again, intercession is a serving role that requires submission to the authorities that have been put in place. To rebel against a leader is to rebel against God (Rom. 13:1-2). As intercessors, we want to be aligned with God and not in opposition to Him. We can do very little to impact the spiritual realm without His authority and power. That is why submission and unity are so important. Of course, this does not mean that we follow blindly and obediently if the leader is not leading the team with integrity. If the leader is not leading in a godly way, then the process laid out in Matthew 18 should be followed with a focus to resolve the problems and restore team unity. We must be wise and ultimately submitted to God's Word and His purposes. Our goal is to honor God and His will.

Unified with Fellow Team Members

Likewise, we must be in unity with one another. Offense is one of the greatest weapons of the enemy to destroy our effectiveness as Christians. If we carry offense for another member of the team, our prayers may become tainted. As discussed previously, conflicts should be resolved quickly and completely, following the example of Jesus. He has forgiven us of all our sins, and we should do likewise with those who have offended us. Only then will the team be unified. James 1:19-20 states, *"My dear brothers and sisters, take note of this: Everyone should be quick to listen, slow to speak and slow to become angry, because human anger does not produce the righteousness that God desires."*

As intercessors, we must be able to "see" God to know what He is doing so we can partner with Him to accomplish His will. Offense and unforgiveness will blind us and keep us from being effective because we will be praying from our own fleshly wisdom and brokenness. Hebrews 12:15 reminds us that offense is often not a private matter that only affects us and our offender. It can, and often will, impact other people around us if left unresolved. *"See to it that no one falls short of the grace of God and that no bitter root grows up to cause trouble and defile many."* Unresolved offense has a way of contaminating those around us and defiling them in our issues. I have often witnessed someone who has been offended talking about the offense with everyone and anyone except the person who offended them. This type of gossip or unholy talk is often done to gain support for the offended person's position. They are craving validation and trying to cultivate opposition against the offender. Whether this is done intentionally or unintentionally, the results are the same. Division develops, and the door is opened for the enemy to infiltrate the church. This is the opposite of what an intercessor should be trying to accomplish.

Unified with Church Leadership

We must also be in unity with the ministry or church we are serving. If we are upset with the direction the pastor is taking, how can we lovingly and sincerely support the church with our prayers? It is amazingly easy to pray soulish prayers when we are not aligned with the ministry we are serving. What is a soulish prayer? It is when we try to influence God or others to act in support of our own desires instead of following God's will. A soulish prayer might sound something like this: "Lord, please show our senior pastor the error of his ways that he may fire the new worship pastor because the music is too loud." Obviously, this is a bit of a cheeky example, but you get the point. Our offense often clouds our prayers to become more about our preferences and opinions than God's will and purposes. It would be better to step away from the role of intercessor until you can deal with your offense than continue to pray from a place of soulishness or disagreement.

Unified with God

Unity with God is also a key factor for intercession. Do we have unconfessed sin? Are we carrying bitterness? Have we neglected to make time to spend with God in our quiet place? These sorts of things will put us at a distance to God. We will not be unified with His heart and purposes because our thoughts and focus will be on other things. In its simplest form, intercession is watching and listening to God and agreeing with what He is saying and doing through our prayers of declaration. We cannot do that if we are not unified with Him. Many times, we judge God because He has not acted how we thought He should act or responded in our timing. Our judgment causes us to see God through a faulty perspective. What we believe about God will shape how we pray to Him. When we carry judgment in our hearts toward God, we will not pray from a position of understanding His true character of love, mercy, and goodness. We may begin to see Him as harsh, aloof, or unfair. We should make every effort to align ourselves with God because we are virtually helpless without His empowerment of our prayers. Aligning our will with God's will means repentance, confession, and forgiveness at times.

Jesus is always the best example to follow. In the garden of Gethsemane, Jesus prayed, *"Father, if you are willing, take this cup from me; yet not my will, but yours be done"* (Luke 22:42). This is an honest prayer. Jesus did not want to endure the torture, pain, and death of the cross, but He was unified with the Father. He submitted Himself to the Father's will and obediently went to the cross, putting His own desires to the side. As intercessors, we must always be looking to God for direction as we pray. He knows better than we do, and the more we agree and align with Him, the more powerful and effective our prayers will become.

A key to powerful intercession is to be unified with God so closely that we know His will. 1 John 5:14-15 illustrates this clearly. *"This is the confidence we have in approaching God: that if we ask anything according to his will, he hears us. And if we know that he hears us—whatever we ask—we know that we have what we asked of him."* If we know His will, we can pray in agreement with Him. This assures us that our prayers will be answered. If we are aligned with His will, we can ask anything, and it will be done. That means we can pray for divine healing, and the person will be healed. We can ask for His provision to satisfy our significant needs, and they will be met. However, we must know God's will first. When we pray in agreement with His will, there are no limits to what He can do for us and through us (Eph. 3:20).

A few years ago, God clearly put on my heart that our intercessory team needed an extended time of repentance before Him. For about six weeks, the intercessors and I would spend our sessions on our knees and face before God. We repented on behalf of ourselves and the church for hours at a time. I am sure the team came to dread the night we met. I would instruct them to get on the floor and pray for repentance, which was challenging and physically painful, but the breakthrough that came afterward was incredible. Our church saw an increase in physical healings, salvations, and other moves of God that we had not seen before. This team of intercessors modeled unity as they humbly submitted to my direction as the leader and demonstrated loving service to our church community. They were aligned with one another in this season and served our church faithfully. I hate to think what we would have missed in that season had we not been unified.

If you are part of a team already, or are trying to form one for your church, I cannot emphasize strongly enough how important team unity is. It is not easy to cultivate, but it is essential for an intercessory prayer team. It must be the foundation on which you are built. If you have been hurt or offended, please take the time today to resolve that between you, your offender, and God. You will find a new freedom and power in your prayers when you operate in a spirit of unity with other believers and God. Often, the unity of the team determines the effectiveness of your prayers to bring God's will and kingdom to earth.

2

THE DISPLACEMENT PRINCIPLE

In the movie *The Waterboy*, there is a character who blames the devil for everything she does not like or understand. She uses that point of view to keep her son from experiencing a healthy social life as he is growing up. His life was stagnated by his fear of the devil. It was comical in the movie, but I have met many Christians who seem to have a serious problem of seeing a demon behind every bush. It is a unique Christian phenomenon. I have also witnessed many of my team members and others being significantly aware of the enemy's presence while being totally unaware of what God was doing. Why is it that many Christians, especially those who are spiritually young or immature in their faith, find it much easier to perceive the works of the enemy than the works of God? I believe it is because Satan works overtly to create fear in believers and distract us from our focus on God.

Often, intercessors are aware of the presence of darkness long before they are aware of God's presence. I have seen this repeatedly during intercession sessions. An intercessor will perceive some darkness in the room and quickly share the information in the hope that we can confront the enemy and send him away, eager to rush into spiritual warfare without looking to God to see how He is working in the room. This is not necessarily the wrong approach, and I am not here to criticize the sincerity of the effort, but I also know that it is often a subtle scheme of the enemy to wear us down in a spiritual battle. Sometimes a direct approach is appropriate, but I have learned that there is a better way to fight dark spiritual forces and strategies.

Intercessors do need to understand that they are in a spiritual battle (Eph. 6:12), and that we are called to fight the schemes of the enemy. However, there is a danger in approaching spiritual warfare with a solitary focus on what the enemy is doing, and then trying to counteract it. Such a frontal attack can become a laborious and exhausting process. When we give too much attention to the enemy, we can easily lose our focus on God. Fear and confusion can set in. Why let Satan lure us to the battlefield when we should stay in the sanctuary? It is not counterintuitive to conduct spiritual warfare from the sanctuary instead of the battlefield. From many years of experience, I can say that we are much more effective when we fight from God's presence than by our own strength.

Now let's look at the principle of displacement, which is based on John 1:5. *"The light shines in the darkness, and the darkness has not overcome it."* That light is Jesus, Who is the light of the world. He has overcome darkness and defeated Satan through His sacrifice on the cross. In John 8:12, Jesus declared, *"I am the light of the world. Whoever follows me will never walk in darkness but will have the light of life."* As we obediently follow Jesus, we walk in His light. We are His spiritual torch bearers, exposing darkness wherever we tread. When we face darkness, it is not an equal fight because the light of Jesus immediately displaces the darkness.

The displacement principle is simple, but powerful. Wherever darkness is operating, we introduce God's light, which removes the darkness. A simple analogy is what happens when we flip a light switch in a dark room. Unless the switch is malfunctioning or the bulb is burned out, the room immediately fills with light, forcing the darkness to dissipate. Darkness cannot overcome light. The same is true in the spiritual realm. When we are confronted with spiritual darkness, bringing the light of Christ to bear overcomes the darkness.

Scientifically, we understand that darkness is not a tangible substance. It is not made of something you or I can hold or measure. Darkness is simply the absence of light. It is hollow and empty and does not contain weight or volume.

Light, on the other hand, is made of energy that travels as waves of photons. It fills an area and may even bring warmth. Because light is made of energy, it contains power. Spiritually, darkness operates in spaces where the light [of Christ] is absent; in places where we have believed lies or allowed fear to override our faith. Introducing the light of Jesus by declaring His truth and promises removes or displaces spiritual darkness.

For example, an intercessor may perceive a spirit of fear over a person or group. The way to displace the spirit of fear is to introduce the opposite spiritual force, which is love (1 John 4:13-18, 2 Tim. 1:7). Instead of praying against the spirit of fear directly, ask God to release His love over the person or group. Pray that the room be filled with God's overwhelming love. If appropriate, demonstrate love by giving the person a hug. As we experience God's perfect love, fear is driven away. The darkness cannot resist the light of Christ and must leave. Because most darkness is operating in some form of a lie or deception, the light of Jesus exposes the works of the enemy so they can be removed and replaced with the purposes of God. The key is to stay focused on God, His Word, and the truth.

Keep Your Eyes Fixed on God

The beauty of the displacement principle is that it keeps our eyes focused. When our prayers remain centered on the truth of God's Word and the promises He has made to us, His children, we will stay focused on what God is saying and doing instead of getting distracted by what the enemy is doing. Paul tells us in Philippians 4:8 to keep our minds focused on what is pure, good, and lovely. *"Finally, brothers and sisters, whatever is true, whatever is noble, whatever is right, whatever is pure, whatever is lovely, whatever is admirable—if anything is excellent or praiseworthy—think about such things."* When we pray from the light of Jesus, we do not have to focus on the enemy. With this proper focus, our prayers become declarations of God's goodness, which is a superior spiritual warfare strategy.

Jesus has already overcome all darkness. The displacement principle enables us to apply this reality to any situation we are faced with. Colossians 3:1-2 tells us, *"Since, then, you have been raised with Christ, set your hearts on things above, where Christ is, seated at the right hand of God. Set your minds on things above, not on earthly things."* This approach is much better than trying to forcibly confront darkness head-on. The head-on approach can shift our focus to the works of the enemy and earthly things instead of looking to heaven where Christ is seated, ready to give us strategies for warfare. When we combat the spiritual forces of darkness from God's presence and His perspective, we can remain in a place of rest instead of exhausting ourselves. I have seen this principal work time and time again, and I can tell you that it makes spiritual warfare much more effective.

I have found that intercession is remarkably like deliverance ministry because of the aspect of spiritual warfare. My background as a pastor was in deliverance ministry, which is where the displacement principle emerged. I was always looking for ways to speed up the process of deliverance and healing. Declaring truth is often the beginning of freedom for a demonized individual. The declaration of truth introduces light to the dark lies that Satan has sown in a person's thinking. The enemy is a liar and uses lies to infiltrate our thoughts and beliefs. When these lies become ingrained in our identity, resulting behavior patterns give Satan authority to influence our lives.

In intercession, when we use the displacement principle, we declare through our prayers what is true (light), and that truth replaces the lies (darkness). This is praying from the reality of heaven instead of praying from our earthly circumstances. Praying from the reality of heaven brings a quick shift in the spiritual atmosphere because we are partnering with God from the heavenly realm instead of trying to fight the lies of Satan in the earthly realm. Scripture tells us that God has given us spiritual weapons to defeat our spiritual enemy. *"For though we live in the world, we do not wage war as the world does. The weapons we fight with are not the weapons of the world. On the contrary, they have divine power to demolish strongholds"* (2 Cor. 10:3-4). When we intercede over a person or situation, we release divine power that destroys the works of the enemy because light always triumphs over darkness.

Satan does not want to confront us on a spiritual level because he has already lost the battle there. He tries to lure us into fighting against him on an earthly level where he has superior assets.

Our initial perception of a situation or circumstance is often made by what we are seeing, feeling, and experiencing. This is our earthly reality. There is a superior parallel reality in the spiritual realm where God is operating. We must train ourselves to look to God to determine our ultimate reality and what is true. For instance, we may be feeling lonely, but God promises never to leave or forsake us (Deut. 31:6). The greater spiritual reality tells us that we are never alone, even though we may have feelings of loneliness in our earthly reality. Using the displacement principle, we can shift those feelings of loneliness by applying and believing the spiritual reality that God is always with us. It is important to learn to discern the difference between earthly circumstances and the reality of heaven.

Intercession differs from deliverance ministry because the intercessor is usually praying over a group of people and sensing what is going on in the spiritual realm around them. They are often dealing with the spiritual environment or dynamic of the room and not a specific spirit operating in or around a person. However, the spiritual battle is no less real or challenging. It requires a full reliance on the Holy Spirit and a strong knowledge of God's Word. We must be in tune with the Holy Spirit because He is the one who will reveal where the enemy is trying to deceive us in our earthly circumstances or experiences. When we counter these lies with the truth, our feelings and perceptions will become aligned with the reality of heaven, and our dark circumstances will be overcome by the light of God.

God's Word is Powerful

To use the displacement principle, an intercessor must know how to pray in an opposite spirit to the darkness they are confronting. This requires a mature biblical knowledge. We must know what God's Word says and how to apply it to the situation at hand. The Holy Spirit is our helper and is always faithful to reveal how to pray if we are listening and submitted to Him. You may not know that the spiritual opposite of fear is love (1 John 4:18), or you may think courage is the opposite of fear, but things are different in the spiritual realm. Therefore, we must keep our eyes fixed on Jesus and not on our earthly circumstances.

Sometimes it is obvious how to pray. For example, if there is a sense of hopelessness, we would pray for hope. If we have strong biblical knowledge, no matter what the enemy is doing, we have an answer for it from the Bible. If you serve as an intercessor, spend time reading God's Word every day so you are filled with God's truth and can rebut the lies of the enemy. Jesus demonstrated this power as He refuted Satan's temptations in the wilderness (Matt. 4:1-11) using the light of scripture to reveal the dark lies hidden in Satan's temptations. Satan could not argue with the truth and inevitably had to leave, defeated by Jesus.

The enemy cannot argue against God's Word. When we intercede by quoting scripture, God's power is attached to our prayers. Because His Word contains power, when our scriptural prayers align us with His truth, our words are empowered to apply God's authority. *"For the word of God is alive and active. Sharper than any double-edged sword, it penetrates even to dividing soul and spirit, joints and marrow; it judges the thoughts and attitudes of the heart"* (Heb. 4:12). The truth of the Bible reveals Satan's lies to be false and removes his power to deceive us. Remember, Satan's work is always empowered by lies (John 8:44). The displacement principle counters Satan's lies with God's truth. We simply introduce light, and the darkness must flee. In this way, we are not only engaging in spiritual warfare, but we are partnering with Jesus, Who is the light of the world. We are walking in His light, illuminating our world with every step we take.

Partnering with the Holy Spirit

In addition to knowing God's Word and applying it in intercession, we must also be looking and listening to the Holy Spirit. This is an intentional step when using the displacement principle. I opened this chapter by commenting on how easy it is to see the works of the enemy. When we sense darkness is present, we often want to respond immediately. It is important not to rush in pursuing the enemy before we are ready for warfare. If we rush into battle without preparing, we are setting ourselves up for a difficult struggle. Before facing Goliath, David prepared himself by collecting five stones for his slingshot. He fought on the battlefield, but not before he armed himself with what he needed. Once we become aware of the plans of the enemy, we must wait on God to reveal His plans and partner with His strategies. This comes through the revelation of the Holy Spirit. *"Or suppose a king is about to go to war against another king. Won't he first sit down and consider whether he is able with ten thousand men to oppose the one coming against him with twenty thousand?"* (Luke 14:31).

As Christians, we carry the presence, the light, and the authority of Jesus within us through the Holy Spirit. What is in us is greater than the darkness of the world (1 John 4:4). Our intercession becomes powerful when we conduct spiritual warfare from the presence of the One who has already overcome the darkness. In His presence, we can clearly hear His voice and declare His truth. Intimacy with the Father through the Holy Spirit gives us a familiarity with His ways, enabling us to recognize the counterfeit and avoid falling prey to the lies of the enemy. We must tune our ears to His voice to hear what He is saying. What is His will for the people we are interceding for? When we wait for His direction and partner with Him in agreement, our prayers become much more powerful and effective. In essence, our prayers will be aligned with His will, and He will answer us (1 John 5:14-15). God is always active (Ps. 121). We must become more aware of what God is doing than what Satan is doing by spiritually watching and listening. If Satan is working in a situation, know that God is working in that same situation.

Watch and Listen

The displacement principle works best when we are praying from the reality of heaven (what God is saying and doing) and releasing that reality on earth. The signs, wonders, and miracles that occurred throughout the ministry of Jesus came about because Jesus was always watching the Father and acting in obedience. *"Very truly I tell you, the Son can do nothing by himself; he can do only what he sees his Father doing, because whatever the Father does the Son also does"* (John 5:19). As we watch and listen to the Father, agree with His will, and act in obedience, we too will see God move through our intercession. God's heavenly authority always displaces the authority of Satan on earth when we obediently partner with Him. If we are not watching and listening, we will not know what God is doing and thus, we will not be able to partner with His will as we pray.

At one point in history, Satan had authority over the earth, and he demonstrated this authority when he tempted Jesus in the wilderness. *"Again, the devil took him to a very high mountain and showed him all the kingdoms of the world and their splendor. 'All this I will give you,' he said, 'if you will bow down and worship me'"* (Matt. 4:8-9). Satan offered Jesus authority over all the kingdoms of the world if Jesus would worship him. He [Satan] could not offer this to Jesus if it did not belong to him. Satan had authority over the earth, but only for a limited time. Jesus would eventually take this authority from Satan through His death and resurrection. After His resurrection and before He ascended to heaven, Jesus declared that He had taken back the authority over the earth. *"Then Jesus came to them and said, 'All authority in heaven and on earth has been given to me'"* (Matt. 28:18).

As believers and intercessors, it is so important to remember that Jesus now has the authority over heaven and earth, and as His children, we carry His authority and can apply it when we pray. The only authority that Satan has now is what we give him through sin, lies, doubt, and fear. The displacement principle operates in spiritual authority, and works so well that when we apply Jesus' authority, it nullifies the authority Satan is operating in. The light of Jesus shines in the darkness, and the darkness cannot overcome it.

The displacement principle is simple in concept, but powerful in application. It requires the intercessor to be close to God to hear His voice and see His hand at work. Keep your eyes fixed on Jesus and do not become fearful at the presence of darkness around you. Wait on Him, and you will understand His plans. You carry the light of Jesus within you that has overcome all darkness. Applying the authority of Jesus through the displacement principle will negate the plans of the enemy and release the blessings of heaven, bringing heaven to earth.

And this is my prayer: that your love may abound more and more in knowledge and depth of insight, so that you may be able to discern what is best and may be pure and blameless for the day of Christ, filled with the fruit of righteousness that comes through Jesus Christ—to the glory and praise of God.

— PHILIPPIANS 1:9-11

3

UNDERSTANDING THE PRINCIPLES OF SPIRITUAL AUTHORITY PART 1

As an avid baseball fan, I have always been entertained by the dynamic between the home plate umpire and the batter. The home plate umpire's primary responsibility is to call balls and strikes against the batter. If the batter receives three strikes, he is out. There is an established strike zone between the knees and chest of a batter over the dimensions of the home plate, but sometimes that strike zone can be stretched or compressed based on how the umpire judges a pitch. There are unwritten rules for how a batter can complain about a call and not get thrown out of the game. If a batter disagrees with the umpire's call, they will often mumble their protest while looking away from the umpire. They use body language to express their disagreement. This passive opposition is usually overlooked.

Occasionally, the batter might try to confront the umpire

directly and let them know that they strongly disagree. This is where it can get entertaining. There is no video replay for the calls at the plate, and so the authority of the umpire is supreme. Rebelling against a call often results in the player being ejected from the game after a heated debate. It does not matter whether you agree or disagree with the umpire—his decisions are final. His authority will be enforced. In baseball, the person with the authority has the power. This is true in the spiritual realm as well.

In Western culture today, the word "authority" is often understood negatively. It is a word that represents oppression, and we do not like to feel weak or powerless. Many people do not want to be told what to do and rebel against the authorities in their lives. Those in authority often misuse their power to take advantage of the position they possess, creating an unfair dynamic between themselves and those they lead. Consequently, many do not trust what the authorities have to say. I believe it has brought us to a place where many people think they themselves should be the only authority they need to follow. This has caused us as a society to experience significant consequences. There have been far too many news stories in recent years depicting people rebelling in violent and destructive ways because they refuse to submit to authority.

Authority is not a bad thing. In fact, all authority is designated by God, the ultimate authority over the universe. You might say He is the universal home plate umpire. As a Christian, and especially as an intercessor, we must understand how to operate in our own authority while operating under the authority that has been placed over us in the spiritual and earthly realms. Without an understanding of authority, we can put ourselves in a dire position.

Authority Dictates Everything in the Spiritual Realm

In the spiritual realm, everything is dictated by authority, and every spiritual being can only operate within the parameters of their designated authority. Spiritual authority does not necessarily mean being "in charge." It is about being empowered to operate in a particular way. It is about enforcing a particular outcome or situation. Nothing happens in the spiritual realm without authority being given or acquired. Obviously, God is the ultimate authority. He is in control, but there are many degrees of authority operating under His throne. Just as an earthly president or king may have authority over a country, there are also many other positions of authority operating under the ruler.

Some authority has been given or appointed by God, and some authority has been stolen by Satan. In the last chapter, I explained that Satan once had authority over the earth and operated in that authority freely. Upon Christ's death and resurrection, that authority was taken from Satan and given to Jesus. Therefore, Jesus now has the authority of heaven and earth, which means that Satan and his kingdom can only operate in the authority they have acquired through our sin and fear.

Spiritual Hierarchies

A straightforward way to understand how spiritual authority operates is to compare it to a military structure. Within the military, there are ranks, and each rank carries a certain degree of power. For instance, a general has a significant amount of authority within the military hierarchy. Generals make decisions and give out orders for lower ranks to follow. Those under a general's authority must do what he commands. The general's commands empower the lower ranks to operate toward a desired outcome or goal. There are consequences if any lower rank refuses to follow the general's command. A sergeant has more authority than a private, but less authority than a captain. Even a general is bound by the authority structure.

Each rank can only operate in the authority it has been given for the military to function with order and effect. Without this structure, the whole organization would be thrown into chaos, and the defense of our country would not be possible. A general's authority is limited by the government that employs him as well as by the military branch that he serves. An Army general does not have the authority to command the Navy, and an Admiral cannot command the Air Force. Every aspect of the military is dictated by the authority structure, which allows it to function as it should. The spiritual realm operates in a similar fashion, and although it can be quite complex, authority is the dictating factor in the spiritual realm.

Ephesians 6 is one of the clearest examples of the hierarchy of spiritual authority. Paul writes,

---

Put on the full armor of God, so that you can take your stand against the devil's schemes. For our struggle is not against flesh and blood but against the rulers, against the authorities, against the powers of this dark world and against the spiritual forces of evil in the heavenly realms.

— EPHESIANS 6:11-12

Paul takes the time to mention several levels of authority within the spiritual and earthly realm where Satan and his kingdom operate. Paul names rulers, authorities, powers, and spiritual forces of evil. Each of these designations carry different degrees of authority and rule. Some are in the spiritual realm, and some are in the earthly realm. They have obtained these positions through the fallenness of our world and acquire their strength through our sin and fear. Paul does not explain the hierarchy of spiritual authority in detail, but he does gives us enough information to understand that it does exist.

As a deliverance minister, I have seen spiritual hierarchies of authority operating in an individual. Often, there is an initial demon that gains authority in a person's life and then continues to bring in other subordinate demons to entrench themselves and supplement the original demon's position and purpose. Remember, spiritual authority is not always about being in charge, but is an empowerment to operate in a specific way. An individual who has been demonized is not fully and completely possessed. They are not controlled by the demon in every area of their life. The demon has authority to influence and impact a person in specific ways, which may have significant impact, but is not in total control of the person. If a person is viewed as a metaphorical house, the area of demonic influence may consist of a small cabinet or closet. They may also have influence over an entire floor, but they do not control the entire house.

Here is a hypothetical example of how it works. If a person experiences significant trauma as a child, that trauma often creates fear, which may allow a spirit of fear to enter the child. Once entrenched, the spirit of fear begins to work to exacerbate all the normal fears a child may experience so they become extreme fears. No matter how irrational the fears are or how many times the parents try to explain that there is nothing to be afraid of, the child cannot overcome their feelings of fear. As a result, traumatized children can start to feel like there is something wrong with them as the spirit of fear speaks lies to them and tells them they are inadequate or strange.

If the child believes these lies, their belief gives the demonic spirit more authority. All of this can bring a sense of low self-esteem to the child, which in turn introduces a new demon that chips away at the child's sense of worth and identity. This new demon is under the authority of the spirit of fear and works in cooperation with it, keeping the child in an environment of constant insecurity. This pattern can continue until there are multiple demons operating in various areas of a person's life. However, they are all working under the authority of the spirit of fear.

To remove these demons one by one can be a lengthy process. The quickest and best way to cast them out is to start with the demon that holds the most authority. In this case, it is the spirit of fear. Once this root is discovered, you can remove its authority and bind the subordinate demons to it and then cast the whole lot out at once. If you remove the king, the kingdom will fall. Finding the root of authority is the key.

This example demonstrates that there are degrees of authority operating in the spiritual realm. The demons that operate within or around an individual tend to be the "privates" in Satan's army. They do not have significant strength or authority except what they have acquired through sin and fear. Once a person has forgiven, repented, renounced, or broken ties with the fear and lies of the demonic, the spirits must go because they no longer hold authority over the person. In this example, the lie that the child may have believed is that they are always unsafe. If the child believes this lie, it gives the spirit of fear authority to oppress the child. Once the lie is refuted and the truth revealed, the spirit of fear's authority is negated. The Christian can then stand in the authority of Jesus and tell the spirit or spirits to go. The spirits must obey because they are beings that operate exclusively under authority. Once their authority has been negated, they must submit to and obey the new, superior authority.

You may be wondering how these satanic authorities have power if Jesus took back all authority in heaven and earth. What is important to understand is that their authority has not been given; it has been acquired. In fact, you could say that it has been stolen. The satanic kingdom no longer has authority in the earthly or spiritual realm except what has been given over to them through humanity's sin and fear. Sin and fear are the resources that the enemy needs to have authority to operate, and demonic spirits often acquire this through lies and deception. Just as Satan deceived Eve in the garden of Eden, he tries to deceive individuals today so that he may acquire authority over us. We empower the things that we agree with. When we believe the lies of the enemy, we give Satan power to rule over us. It is not complete authority and control, but if we allow the enemy to continue to work unimpeded, he can gain a considerable influence in our life.

The Chained Elephant

You may have heard the story of the chained elephant. A boy goes to a circus and becomes enamored by the elephants in the show. He is impressed by how large and powerful they are. After the show, the boy wants to see the elephants up close. As he tours the circus grounds, he is saddened to see the other beautiful animals locked in cages unable to run free. When he gets to the elephants, he is surprised to see them out in the open. Being such powerful creatures, he is astonished that the only thing preventing them from running away is a small chain attached to one leg and staked in the ground. The boy wonders why such large, strong animals do not simply pull the stake out and run free. This question consumes his thoughts as he seeks the answer from his parents and others to no avail. He eventually discovers that the elephants were trained to stay put when they were small and weak. The trainers chain the elephant to a stake while it is still a baby and not strong enough to free itself. The baby elephant may exhaust itself pulling against the stake but cannot get free, eventually deciding that it is pointless to strain against the restraint, believing it is trapped. As the elephant grows, it does not realize that the chain and stake are no longer able to hold it captive, so it obediently stays in place.

This is an analogy of how Satan gains authority over us. He sells us a lie that we are chained to a sin or circumstance so powerful that we will never be free. He often uses negative experiences from our childhood to ingrain that lie in our thinking. All of this is so we come to believe that we are helpless. The truth is that Jesus has forgiven sin and dealt with it on the cross for those who are believers. He has the power and authority to heal the emotional and spiritual wounds of the past. Sadly, too many believe the lies of Satan and obediently remain chained to a simple stake in the ground, unable to enjoy the gift of freedom available from Jesus at salvation (Gal. 5:1). When we agree with the lies of the enemy, we empower him to hold us captive. Just like the elephant, we have the strength and ability to be free, but because we believe the lies of Satan, we remain captive as we have given Satan authority to rule over an aspect of our life. As Christians, Jesus has given us the authority to break every chain and live free (Rom. 6:20-23). One role of an intercessor is to break the chains of authority that Satan is using to limit the church. We do this by exposing his lies with the light of truth.

Angelic Hierarchies

The hierarchy of spiritual authority is not limited only to dark spiritual entities. The angelic also has a hierarchy. Although there is not a large amount of information about angelic hierarchies included in the Bible, there are a few passages that hint at an authority structure. In Jude 9, Michael is called an archangel. *"But even the archangel Michael, when he was disputing with the devil about the body of Moses, did not himself dare to condemn him for slander but said, 'The Lord rebuke you!'"* The designation of "archangel" infers that Michael held a position of leadership over other angels. It also demonstrates that Michael realizes that his authority pales in comparison to the authority of the Lord. Instead of rebuking the devil directly, he invokes God's authority to rebuke Satan.

In Daniel, Michael is called "one of the chief princes." *"Then Michael, one of the chief princes, came to help me, because I was detained there with the king of Persia"* (Dan. 10:13b). In Revelation 12:7-8, Michael leads an angelic army against Satan. *"Then war broke out in heaven. Michael and his angels fought against the dragon, and the dragon and his angels fought back."* These limited sources give us another glimpse into the structures of authority operating in the spiritual realm. Michael obviously holds a higher rank than other angels, but is also under the authority of God.

The Authority of Jesus

As intercessors, we operate in the authority of Jesus. He sits at the right hand of God and has authority over all other authorities. 1 Peter 3:21-22 tells us, *"...Jesus Christ, who has gone into heaven and is at God's right hand— [He now rules] with angels, authorities and powers in submission to him."* During His ministry on earth, Jesus gave His disciples authority to do God's will. *"When Jesus had called the Twelve together, he gave them power and authority to drive out all demons and to cure diseases, and he sent them out to proclaim the kingdom of God and to heal the sick"* (Luke 9:1-2). In another instance, Jesus sent out seventy-two disciples to preach the gospel, cast out demons, and heal the sick. Upon their return, they joyfully proclaimed, *"Lord, even the demons submit to us in your name"* (Luke 10:17). Jesus replies, *"I have given you authority to trample on snakes and scorpions and to overcome all the power of the enemy; nothing will harm you"* (Luke 10:19). The only authority we have is what has been given to us by Jesus, and His authority is supreme. He gives us some of His authority that we may do His will and tear down demonic authorities in the world.

Operating in the authority of Jesus is important because as intercessors, we will confront other authorities that are in opposition to Christ's kingdom. If we try to use any other means than the authority of Jesus to pull down demonic strongholds, we will not be successful. It is only by the authority of Jesus that we can overcome darkness. Authority is the greatest weapon of an intercessor.

For though we live in the world, we do not wage war as the world does. The weapons we fight with are not the weapons of the world. On the contrary, they have divine power to demolish strongholds. We demolish arguments and every pretension that sets itself up against the knowledge of God, and we take captive every thought to make it obedient to Christ.

— 2 CORINTHIANS 10:3-5

To be effective as an intercessor, you must understand how authority works. In the same way that a soldier is taught how to clean, hold, and fire his rifle appropriately, we must also learn how to use the spiritual authority of Jesus as a weapon against the enemy.

Operating in Our Authority Structures

Operating in our delegated authority is essential to the ministry of intercession. Intercessors must understand the framework of authority and how to apply it when praying, which means we must understand how to operate *under* authority. If we are unwilling to submit to the authorities that have been placed in our lives in the natural, chances are we might not understand spiritual authority and therefore lose our effectiveness as intercessors. This is an area where many make mistakes and reap unwanted consequences. In the work world, if we either overstep our authority in our job or refuse to fulfill our responsibilities, our disobedience is not without consequences. We might be passed over for promotions or even be fired. Likewise, we must know how to appropriately operate in our spiritual authority structures to be effective and not bring spiritual consequences. Just as we would honor those in authority over us in the workplace, we must honor the spiritual leaders God has placed over us if they are living and acting with honor and integrity.

It is tempting to believe that we can do better than the person in leadership over us. We all have opinions and preferences, and we like to focus on our strengths instead of our weaknesses. Our pride can convince us that we should be the one calling the shots, especially if we are functioning at a higher level in our giftings than those in leadership. This does not give us the right to usurp the authority of those placed over us. No leader is perfect. We all have flaws and insecurities. When those flaws present themselves in someone in leadership, we may want to rebel against that person. We tend to judge others by their actions and judge ourselves by our motives because it is easier to observe and judge someone else's flaws than our own. We tend to minimize our own mistakes, especially when we know that we were trying our best. This is unfair to those in leadership. God honors those who honor authority (Rom. 13:1-3). Hebrews 13:17 encourages us, *"Have confidence in your leaders and submit to their authority, because they keep watch over you as those who must give an account. Do this so that their work will be a joy, not a burden, for that would be of no benefit to you."* It is important to remember that we cannot all be leaders; we need followers too. Each role is significant and carries value. Honoring authority is a biblical concept that we should not overlook or ignore.

The Centurion

In Luke 7, we read the story of a centurion who asks Jesus to heal his servant. This story is a powerful example of a man who understood both spiritual and earthly authority. He had authority and was also subject to authority. His ability to operate within authority structures impressed Jesus.

> *When Jesus had finished saying all this to the people who were listening, he entered Capernaum. There was a centurion's servant, whom his master valued highly, was sick and about to die. The centurion heard of Jesus and sent some elders of the Jews to him, asking him to come and heal his servant. When they came to Jesus, they pleaded*

earnestly with him, "This man deserves to have you do this, because he loves our nation and has built our synagogue." So Jesus went with them. He was not far from the house when the centurion sent friends to say to him: "Lord, don't trouble yourself, for I do not deserve to have you come under my roof. That is why I did not even consider myself worthy to come to you. But say the word, and my servant will be healed. For I myself am a man under authority, with soldiers under me. I tell this one, 'Go,' and he goes; and that one, 'Come,' and he comes. I say to my servant, 'Do this,' and he does it." When Jesus heard this, he was amazed at him, and turning to the crowd following him, he said, "I tell you, I have not found such great faith even in Israel." Then the men who had been sent returned to the house and found the servant well.

— LUKE 7:1-10

There are several things we need to pay attention to in this story. First, the centurion knew his boundaries and remained within them. He was not a man of great spiritual authority despite his great earthly authority. He did not go to Jesus directly, but sent some Jewish elders to speak to Him instead. The centurion would have been a Roman and Jesus was a Jew. The relationship between these two groups would have been tenuous at best. The centurion could have tried to use his authority to forcibly intimidate Jesus to come to his house, but this would have been an abuse of his power. Instead, he humbled himself before Jesus by sending Jewish messengers. As a centurion, he had the power to direct a Jew because Rome ruled over the area. Roman rule was known to be harsh and unjust at times. This centurion seems to be different. Scripture says that the elders declared that he [the centurion] loved the Jews and had helped to build their synagogue. His humble approach was an act of honor toward Jesus. The centurion chose humility over pride in his position.

Secondly, the centurion understood both earthly and spiritual authority. Despite his earthly position, he did not see himself as worthy to welcome Jesus under his roof, recognizing that the authority Jesus carried was far superior to his own. Jesus carried spiritual power to heal the centurion's servant, while the centurion only had earthly authority. He also understood that he was under authority. He gave commands, but he also had to follow orders. Because the centurion understood the earthly hierarchy of authority, he was able to recognize the spiritual authority of Jesus.

Finally, the centurion exercised faith in the authority Jesus carried. Being a man familiar with authority structures, he believed that Jesus could heal his servant simply by giving the word. He recognized that Jesus could command sickness and it would obey just as he commanded his soldiers and servants. Like the centurion, do we have faith in the authority of Jesus? Do we believe He can accomplish miraculous things with just a word?

Our Words Carry Authority

Our words carry authority. Therefore, to honor the authorities in our lives, we must watch what we say. The things that we idly voice, as well as our spoken prayers, carry power. Are you speaking words of encouragement, or are you speaking words of judgment and gossip? When you speak of your church leaders, are your words building them up or tearing them down? The enemy can use your critical tongue to acquire authority to come against those you speak of negatively. Our words can become blessings or curses. *"The tongue has the power of life and death, and those who love it will eat its fruit"* (Prov. 18:21). Those in authority over us have been placed there by God. It is to our benefit to serve them humbly.

Spiritual Umbrellas

In my chapter on the principle of unity, I discussed how honoring the leadership that has been placed over us is vital to our role as intercessors. Leadership carries authority, and we must be willing to serve under that authority to be effective. In fact, serving under authority builds a spiritual covering and empowers our individual authority. It allows us to pray bold and courageous prayers because the relational structures are established. As the pastor of prayer, I was given authority to intercede over my church by individuals who had greater spiritual authority in the church. My senior pastor and the eldership trusted me and gave me the responsibility of forming and leading an intercessory prayer team. Those who served on that team were under my leadership and relied on me to provide spiritual covering for them as we conducted spiritual warfare on behalf of the church. Like a series of spiritual umbrellas, there was a hierarchy of authority that protected us from the storms of the enemy as we prayed. That is why it is so important that we understand where we sit within the structures of spiritual and earthly authority when we serve.

As intercessors, we are primarily praying into the spiritual realm where authority dictates the outcome. If we try to go outside or above our position of authority, we will be operating in rebellion, which makes us more vulnerable to the enemy's attacks because the spiritual covering of our leaders is no longer there. Imagine a soldier deciding to attack the enemy line on his own without the support of the rest of his platoon. He may think that he is doing a brave thing when he is actually acting unwisely and putting himself and possibly others in unnecessary danger. While operating within an authority structure may seem like an inconvenience at times, it is for our benefit and protection spiritually.

Each of us experiences the effects of authority every day. As intercessors, we must understand how spiritual authority operates and how to partner with Jesus to enforce His authority against the dark spiritual forces in the world. Understanding is only the beginning. Once we see how the spiritual realm is organized, it is much easier to know how to apply the authority we have been given by Jesus. The application of authority is where true power is released in the spiritual realm. The next chapter contains a few examples of how the proper and improper application of authority can have dramatic implications in the battle against Satan and his kingdom.

4

UNDERSTANDING THE PRINCIPLES OF SPIRITUAL AUTHORITY PART 2

Apart from God Himself, no one operates in complete autonomous authority. Even Satan is bound by the structures of authority that have been established by God. As intercessors, we must be wise not to step over lines of authority just because we are enthusiastic and willing to breach the gates of hell with a water pistol. Instead, we must be aware of the boundaries of our authority and remain within them. Satan is a legalist, and like a crafty lawyer, he will use the laws of authority to his advantage. What do I mean? I mean we have delegated limits of authority that God has given us to operate within. If we venture beyond these limits, we make ourselves vulnerable to Satan enforcing the laws of authority against us even though we may think we are doing the right thing.

Take law enforcement jurisdictions, for example. In Australia, law enforcement is divided between the states and territories. The authority of the police to enforce the law is limited by the boundary of the state where they serve. They do not have the ability to enter another state or territory to enforce the law because they have not been given authority to operate there. There are times when they receive permission to cross the border, but they cannot do this on their own accord. If they do, they may face consequences. The arrests they make will most likely be thrown out because they did not have the authority to enforce the law in that state. In the same way, God has given us boundaries of authority to operate in, and it is wise to stay within those boundaries.

God has placed each of us in our areas of ministry and given us spiritual authority to operate there. We must know when to engage the enemy as well as which battles are ours to face. When I was given responsibility to form and lead an intercessory prayer team for my church, I was given authority to intercede for the ministries of our church. In that capacity, I served under the authority of the senior pastor and the elders, which gave me confidence to confront any darkness opposing our congregation. I knew that any spiritual warfare that the team and I conducted on behalf of the church was within my boundaries of authority, and therefore God would protect us before, during, and after the battle. We prayed bold prayers and saw powerful strongholds fall because we were under the authority of the church and remained within our boundaries.

It would not be wise or nearly as effective to pray such

bold prayers over another church that I am not affiliated with because it would be outside my authority. If I am in another church or area outside my spiritual boundaries, I always ask permission to conduct spiritual warfare prayers because I want the covering that comes with that permission. Essentially, I become deputized to conduct spiritual warfare over the church or area by the authorities that have been placed there. For those times that God calls us outside our normal boundaries to intercede, we must be sure He is leading us there.

Poking the Bear

Several years ago, I conducted a prayer ministry session with a person who had recently returned from mission work in Egypt. While there, they visited the great pyramids and the Sphinx. Foolishly, they decided to pray against the Sphinx and all it represented directly. If you are unaware, this is the place where many witchcraft and pagan practices originated. The powers that operate there are formidable. This person was not Egyptian and was not interceding at the request of anyone in Egypt. They had impulsively taken on strong spiritual authorities that were outside their personal boundaries of authority. The consequences of this decision resulted in severe demonic attack and oppression, which required extensive prayer ministry because this missionary had not been given permission to oppose such a strong demonic authority. This is what I call "poking the bear."

"Poking the bear" is when someone steps outside their boundaries of authority. In a natural sense, most people would not intentionally provoke a bear because they know that the bear is much bigger and stronger than they are, and it would be unwise to pick a fight with a bear. Unfortunately, many Christians intentionally poke spiritual bears, unaware that their actions may carry consequences, and are then surprised when the spiritual bear mauls them. Authority is a serious matter. We must not let our enthusiasm supersede our obedience to the boundaries God has established. It is especially important to understand our delegated authority and remain within its boundaries if we want to be effective as intercessors. There are times when God extends our boundaries for His purposes, and when that happens, He equips us and empowers us for the battle.

My Japanese Adoption

In 2012, I was invited to participate in mission work in Japan. I had never been there, so I was excited to be a part of the team. Japan is primarily a Buddhist country with a secular government and strongly entrenched spiritual strongholds. Less than one percent of the country identifies as Christian. Currently, there are about 126 million Japanese people in that country, making it one of the largest unreached people groups in the world.

When I arrived in Japan for the first time, I could feel the spiritual heaviness of the people. Although Japan is a rich and thriving country with all the technology and comforts you could want, the people are time-poor, over-worked, and life there is not always easy, hence the exhausted heaviness of the spiritual atmosphere. Despite the spiritual obstacles, my first trip to Japan planted a love in my heart for the Japanese people. Evangelism can be quite difficult there, and although I did not know how we were going to make a real impact for Jesus, I believed we had a calling to bring revival to Japan.

I returned to Japan several more times after that initial trip. A Japanese couple from my church was also involved with the mission team. At one point, the Japanese lady received a prophetic word from the Lord telling her that I was her brother and she was my sister. This was a strange word that neither of us understood initially. What was God's intention in calling us brother and sister? I was an American living in Australia, and she was born in Japan. I knew we were part of God's family, a brother and sister in Christ, but I did not understand that God was doing something deeper. Over many months, God began to reveal to me what this strange word meant and why it was significant. He was spiritually adopting me into a Japanese family so I would not be a foreigner trying to reach someone outside my authority. God was calling me to confront the spiritual powers that were there and that required new, extended spiritual boundaries. As strange as it sounds, when I am in Japan, I am Japanese.

The Shogun Story

God began giving me visions and understanding of the spiritual strongholds over Japan that He wanted to tear down. Although I did not always understand what I was seeing, as I shared them with Japanese Christians, they immediately knew what I was talking about. Slowly, each part of the puzzle was revealed. In a time of prayer, I asked the Lord to show me the highest spiritual authority ruling over the country of Japan. Instantaneously I had a picture of a fierce samurai and heard the word "shogun." The spirit I saw was strong and carried a profound sense of confidence as if he had not been challenged in a long time. In his traditional armor and helmet, he was fiercely intimidating. Although his sword was sheathed, his hand rested upon the handle, ready to draw it at a second's notice.

I shared what I had been seeing with my Japanese sister, and she quickly recognized what I was talking about. A shogun was one of the most politically and socially powerful samurais in Japan. In Japan's early history, shoguns operated regionally as the top political authorities. Through research I discovered that some of the more powerful shoguns had outlawed Christianity around the beginning of the 16th century. All Christians were either killed or expelled from Japan at that time. God showed me that these were the events that gave this ruling spirit authority over Japan in the spiritual realm. I decided to continue my historical research to gather more information about this time in Japan's history.

Hideyoshi Toyotomi, the ruling shogun at the time, first killed Christians on February 5, 1597. He had outlawed Christianity ten years earlier, but due to their small number, Christians were mostly tolerated. As the number of Christians continued to grow, Toyotomi became worried that this new faith would disrupt his desire for a unified Japan, so he executed twenty-six believers to make an example of them. Christianity was a foreign religion that did not align with the Japanese culture. Toyotomi saw Christianity as an obstacle to the unity he was trying to establish because Christians followed God as their ultimate authority and not the shoguns. Unfortunately for Toyotomi, he did not live long enough to see a unified Japan. He died a few months after he executed these Christians, and his successor, Tokugawa Ieyasu, took power.

Toyotomi and his successor, Ieyasu, are heralded in Japan as they brought an era of peace and organization to their nation. This is commonly known as the Edo period. This period of Japanese history is significant because Japan unified as a nation under one leader. Ieyasu continued what Toyotomi started, officially banning all Christian activity in 1614, which resulted in great persecution among Japanese believers. His family ruled Japan in isolation for about 250 years.

There is a famous shrine in Japan called the Nikko Toshogu Shrine, erected in honor of Tokugawa Ieyasu. His remains are entombed in a mausoleum within the shrine. This shrine is especially important to Japan as a national and world landmark site. All Japanese students visit the shrine during their schooling to bow down and pay respect to Ieyasu's accomplishments. Inside this shrine is what is believed to be the original wood carving of the three wise monkeys that hear no evil, speak no evil, and see no evil. You have probably seen a photo, sculpture, or T-shirt depicting these monkeys at some point. They have become a popular image in modern times. The pictorial maxim they present has often been interpreted to mean that we should focus on the positive and ignore the negative. Most people understand the three wise monkeys as something of proverbial wisdom. I learned they represent something completely different.

The Secret of the Three Wise Monkeys

While on a visit to Japan, I met a British man who had been living there for over twenty years. He was a strong Christian and passionate intercessor. When I shared with him what I had seen in my vision, he explained why God had shown me the shogun. Ieyasu was responsible for closing off Japan to Christianity for over 200 years. It was only in the late 19th century that Christians were allowed to share the gospel again and worship without fear of persecution or death. As we talked, he helped me understand what God had been showing me, adding a particularly important part of the story regarding the three monkeys. They have much greater significance than being a cute reminder to avoid evil.

The "evil" that the monkeys are not hearing, speaking, or seeing is Christianity. Ieyasu saw Christianity as the primary opposition to his unification of Japan and condemned it. He wanted this foreign religion eradicated completely from Japan. The three wise monkeys were a clever way to remind the people to avoid Christianity by turning away from hearing, seeing, or speaking the gospel. The three monkeys covertly demonstrate that the gospel was all but totally removed from Japanese culture. The result of this maxim has had terrible spiritual implications over Japan, bringing a curse on the nation that rendered Japan's people unable to hear the good news, speak the praises of God, or see God at work in their lives. The Japanese people had become deaf, blind, and mute to the gospel because of the sins of the shoguns. Their actions had empowered a strong spiritual authority to operate over the country for over 300 years. This British intercessor received this insight from God through many hours spent in prayer with other intercessors. With this knowledge, we began praying for eyes, ears, mouths, and hearts to be opened that God might bring revival to Japan. I believe more intercession is needed, but God is doing something new in Japan!

As I recall this story, I am reminded of God's faithfulness and His greatness. His perspective is so much greater than ours, and He knew the parts of the puzzle that I needed to intercede for Japan at that time. Had God not adopted me into the Japanese family, I would not have had the authority to confront the Japanese ruling spirit. God gave me special authority, and little by little, revealed how we should pray. In recent years, we have seen amazing things happen in Japan for Christ's kingdom. There have been wombs opened and babies born, multiple salvations, physical healings, and favor in schools, shopping malls, and other secular places to share the gospel with the people of Japan. Churches are beginning to grow. If God had not shown my Japanese sister that I was her brother, I would not have attempted to confront such powerful authorities. I know that there are many Christians and intercessors tirelessly praying for revival in Japan, and I am grateful for the grace to be a small part of what God is doing there.

Authority Matters

My experience as an intercessor in Japan is unique, as God clearly called me into that battle. I was cautious and took my time to understand the situation before I proceeded to intercede. It would have been unwise to start praying against the shogun immediately after I saw him in my vision because I did not understand what he represented. I had to wait on the Lord to give me direction to know how to pray, and to do some research as well. It is a good idea to know your opponent before stepping into the ring. I did not confront the shogun directly. Instead, I used the displacement principle and prayed for eyes, ears, and mouths to be opened. I repented on behalf of the Japanese people and the leaders who committed such horrific acts. I would encourage every intercessor to exercise similar caution and take the time to wait on the Lord. It is not about being afraid; it is about being wise. Rushing into spiritual warfare without understanding can lead to significant consequences. One of the best books written on spiritual boundaries of authority is called *Needless Casualties of War* by John Paul Jackson. I highly recommend everyone engaged in spiritual warfare and intercession to read it.

The spiritual authorities we confront are not always as powerful as the shogun. Most of the time, they are operating over a building, geographic area, or someone's home. I have often been asked to pray over someone's home when something does not feel right, or they believe the house is haunted. Haunted buildings are not plagued with ghosts of past residents, as many people believe. The ghosts are not disembodied souls unable to cross over to the afterlife. The strange occurrences that many experience are simply demonic spirits that have gained authority to operate in that structure. When confronted with superior authority through Jesus, they leave these buildings and the haunting ends. Before I spiritually cleanse a house, I always ask permission from the homeowner to conduct spiritual warfare. Even though they have invited me to their home to pray, I specifically ask their permission before I begin praying. The spiritual realm only responds to authority. The spirits you confront know whether or not you have authority, and will either obey or resist you based on that fact. Authority matters, and we must understand how and when to use it effectively.

There was a young couple who had begun to attend our church after moving interstate. They had not yet found a home and were considering staying with the wife's mother in the meantime. This was her childhood home, and it did not carry many pleasant memories. At their request, I visited the home before they moved in to pray over it. The mother was not opposed to having me there, but did not personally request that I pray or directly give me permission. She owned the home and held the spiritual authority over the property. I hesitantly agreed to pray at the request of the son-in-law. He had been the catalyst of my visit that day because he was concerned that it might impact his family negatively if they moved in.

When I entered the house, I could immediately sense there was a lot of darkness present. As I went room to room, I was confronted with spiritual darkness hiding in every corner. It was extremely difficult to shift the darkness because there were so many bad memories of past experiences that remained unresolved and unhealed still lingering there. I spent over three hours praying and casting out darkness until the house finally felt light and free. When I finished praying, I said my goodbyes to the son-in-law.

As soon as I stepped outside the front door, I immediately sensed all the ejected spirits waiting in the front yard. They had obeyed my authority to vacate the rooms of the house, but only while I was there. They were waiting for me to leave so they could return to hiding in their familiar dark corners. They could not resist the authority I carried, but knew the homeowner had not given me implicit permission to remove them. The spirits had to submit to my authority to a degree, but because the actual homeowner was not fully on board with the process, they could not be permanently removed. In the end, I advised against the couple moving in.

Authority matters. It is the primary weapon of an intercessor. We must submit to the authorities that God has placed in our lives as well as applying the authority He has given us. Authority equates to power in the spiritual realm. Our authority is not unlimited, so we must be wise to apply what we have without going outside our established boundaries. God is greater than Satan and He has already won the ultimate victory, and it is important that we remember this simple truth. We will always defeat Satan when we operate in God's authority and by His direction. We must give Jesus praise for defeating the authorities of the world by His sacrifice on the cross. As His dearly loved children, we are now responsible to enforce His authority over the spiritual forces of evil in the world.

Then Jesus came to them and said, "All authority in heaven and on earth has been given to me. Therefore go and make disciples of all nations, baptizing them in the name of the Father and of the Son and of the Holy Spirit, and teaching them to obey everything I have commanded you. And surely I am with you always, to the very end of the age."

— MATTHEW 28:18-20

5

THE PRINCIPLES OF FAITH AND FEAR

Faith and fear are two of the most discussed topics in the Bible. By my count, there are about 458 verses that mention faith and 336 verses that mention fear. Since they are discussed so frequently throughout the Bible, it would benefit every Christian to understand the importance of living from a position of faith versus fear. Both positions carry significant implications for life and ministry. Faith empowers the Christian to live in power and victory. Fear isolates and stagnates a Christian to be ineffective and powerless. Faith and fear can be equally powerful, but with contrasting results. For example, it is faith in Jesus Christ that initially brings us into relationship with God, saving us from our sins (Eph. 2:8). In contrast, the serpent used fear to convince Eve that she was missing out on something as a way to influence her and Adam to disobey God, bringing sin and death into the world (Gen. 3:1-6). Learning to live in faith and to reject the fearful lies of the enemy is essential for intercessors.

As intercessors, we are always dealing with situations that require faith. We must intercede from a position of faith, seeking God's heavenly intervention in our earthly circumstances with complete trust in His ability to impact whatever it is we are praying about. Hebrews 11:6 tells us, *"Without faith it is impossible to please God, because anyone who comes to him must believe that he exists and that he rewards those who earnestly seek him."* It isn't always easy to pray from a position of faith. Problems viewed through our earthly understanding can seem dauting or even impossible. It is faith that enables us to lift our eyes from our earthly viewpoint to look to God, Who has the power and authority to do miraculous things.

Heaven's Reality

When we are in the presence of God, we quickly realize His heavenly reality is vastly different from our earthly reality. Faith empowers our prayers to invite the reality of heaven to invade our reality on earth. Faith exchanges our earthly vision for spiritual vision, enabling us to see the possibilities that are embedded in God's power. Where God rules on His throne, there is no sickness, pain, or sorrow. There are no problems or lack of resources. There is only joy and blessing in His glorious presence. A heavenly invasion results when

God's will is done on earth as it is in heaven. It is faith that engages God's power to heal the sick, restore relationships, and give us victory over the schemes of the enemy working against us. It is from a position of faith that believers can be at perfect peace despite the storms of life that may be raging around us. *"Do not be anxious about anything, but in every situation, by prayer and petition, with thanksgiving, present your requests to God. And the peace of God, which transcends all understanding, will guard your hearts and your minds in Christ Jesus"* (Phil. 4:6-7). A prayer of faith causes our earthly reality to submit to the greater spiritual reality of heaven. It protects our hearts and minds from being infiltrated by fear.

Hebrews 11 reminds us of what God can do through people of faith. After recalling the heroes of faith from past generations, the author of Hebrews expounds on the power of faith:

And what more shall I say? I do not have time to tell about Gideon, Barak, Samson and Jephthath, about David and Samuel and the prophets, who through faith conquered kingdoms, administered justice, and gained what was promised; who shut the mouths of lions, quenched the fury of the flames, and escaped the edge of the sword; whose weakness was turned to strength; and who became powerful in battle and routed foreign armies. Women received back their dead, raised to life again.

— HEBREWS 11:32-35

Do we have the same faith to pray and believe that God can work in the challenges that we face? If we do, God can and will respond in incredible ways.

I believe faith is a supernatural capacity to trust God's ability and character to intervene in our lives despite what our earthly eyes and mind perceive. Hebrews 11:1 describes faith like this: *"Now faith is confidence in what we hope for and assurance about what we do not see."* When faced with problems or challenges, we all hope that God will keep His promise to work all things out for our good (Rom. 8:28). The key is to believe that He is able. It is faith that gives us the confidence that God is working in our favor despite our inability to see the outcome in advance. Hebrews 11:1 reminds us that faith is founded in God's power to work in our lives (what we hope for), and that His character is expressed as a faithful, loving father (assurance about what we do not see). God can do greater things than we can do on our own. It is our faith in Him that releases His power into our lives. God always fulfills His promises to His children; therefore, we can approach Him with faith in our times of need.

Open His Eyes

In 2 Kings, the king of Aram had declared war on Israel. Over and over, he laid a trap to surprise Israel, but the prophet Elisha would warn the king of Israel ahead of time and keep him safe. This happened so often that the king of Aram thought there must be a spy in his army giving away his plans. He soon found out that it was Elisha warning the king of Israel of these attacks. The king of Aram became so frustrated with Elisha that he sent a large group of soldiers and chariots to capture him at the city of Dothan. Overnight, the soldiers and chariots surrounded the city and hemmed in Elisha. When Elisha's servant awoke the next morning, he realized that they were in great danger and became full of fear. The servant was totally focused on what was happening in the earthly realm because he observed the situation through his fleshly understanding. Elisha realized that God had a different plan because he perceived the situation through spiritual eyes. Elisha asked God to open his servant's eyes to see what He was doing.

> "'Don't be afraid,' the prophet answered. 'Those who are with us are more than those who are with them.' And Elisha prayed, 'Open his eyes, Lord, so that he may see.' Then the Lord opened the servant's eyes, and he looked

> *and saw the hills full of horses and chariots of fire all around Elisha."*
>
> — 2 KINGS 6:16-17

Elisha was not fearful like his servant because his focus and faith were on God and not his earthly circumstances.

As intercessors, we must pray in faith. If we are not praying from a position of faith, our prayers can become weak and ineffective. If we do not believe that God can and will respond to our prayers, then why pray at all? Praying without faith can become an exercise in futility. *"But when you ask, you must believe and not doubt, because the one who doubts is like a wave of the sea, blown and tossed by the wind. That person should not expect to receive anything from the Lord. Such a person is double-minded and unstable in all they do"* (James 1:6-8). James tells us not to expect to receive anything from God if we are praying with doubt in our heart. Prayers sprinkled with doubt do not reflect what we say we believe, and can leave us feeling unstable in our relationship with God because they seem to fall on deaf ears. How can we expect such a doubtful prayer to stir the heart of God to action?

In contrast, praying with faith can engage the power of God to move mountains. *"Truly I tell you, if you have faith as small as a mustard seed, you can say to this mountain, 'Move from here to there,' and it will move. Nothing will be impossible for you"* (Matt. 17:20). The key is our faith *in* God, focused on God's power and person while believing that He is the one Who can move mountains for us by His power and authority because we trust in His mighty power to do what we cannot do in our own strength or wisdom. Faith that moves mountains is not about us doing the heavy lifting. It is not some magical energy that empowers us to shift our obstacles like a Jedi using the force. Faith-filled prayers are powerful because they apply God's power and perspective to the situation. Whether we face sickness, trouble, sin, or shame, our prayers of faith will reach God's ears and bring about an answer.

Is anyone among you in trouble? Let them pray. Is anyone happy? Let them sing songs of praise. Is anyone among you sick? Let them call the elders of the church to pray over them and anoint them with oil in the name of the Lord. And the prayer offered in faith will make the sick person well; the Lord will raise them up. If they have sinned, they will be forgiven. Therefore, confess your sins to each other and pray for each other so that you may be healed. The prayer of a righteous person is powerful and effective.

— JAMES 5:13-16

Every believer, not just intercessors, can pray with power and effect if they pray in faith. James encourages us to bring our needs before the Lord. However, he specifically says that our prayers should be offered in faith. We must believe that God can answer our prayer as we pray it. If we pray in faith, our prayers become powerful and effective.

A Special Trip

2020 was a year that challenged the world as we faced a pandemic that touched every continent. Many people suffered through sickness, loss of loved ones, loss of jobs, and forced isolation. For my family, it was a year of exploration and excitement as we got to leave our normal lives behind and travel around Australia. We spent nearly six months in a four-wheel-drive and caravan as we explored the Northern Territory and Far North Queensland. These areas are so remote that the pandemic had minor impact on our ability to move around freely. We were able to take this trip because my wife, Bronwen, had the faith to pray about it for several years in advance. During one particular time of prayer, when she asked God if we could have an extended family trip, she felt that He had responded with a "yes." Admittedly, I was skeptical that it would ever happen when she first brought up the idea. All I could think of were the many reasons why such a trip would be difficult to see come to fruition. Despite my lack of belief, Bronwen continued to pray faithfully that we would be able to take an extended trip as a family, and when she heard His "yes," she took God at His word.

A few months before we were to leave, we received a huge tax bill which took all the money we had saved for the trip, leaving our chances of going on such a long holiday in doubt. Without adequate finances, how could we pay our bills at home as well as pay for the expenses of a multi-month trip? I remember teasing Bronwen with a pious "I told you so," yet none of these issues lessened Bronwen's faith in the slightest. One night during dinner, she explained the situation to us as a family, telling us to watch what God was going to do. Her faith in God's promise to her remained firm despite the numerous obstacles we were facing. It would have been easy to doubt God since we were without adequate finances, I did not have the vacation time approved, and the pandemic was just beginning. She continued to believe nonetheless. Guess what? In a matter of months, we were on the road. God replaced all the finances we had spent on our taxes, and everything came together for us to enjoy this once-in-a-lifetime trip. Bronwen's faith to trust God was rewarded, and the rest of us enjoyed the blessing as well.

Faith is powerful. Prayer is powerful. Prayer from a position of faith can do incredible things! *"Do not be anxious about anything, but in every situation, by prayer and petition, with thanksgiving, present your requests to God"* (Phil. 4:6). I love this verse, as it encourages us to pray about *every* situation. It does not matter whether we are praying about a family trip or for miraculous healing. When we pray in faith, God works in our circumstances. Faith-filled prayer turns the focus from self and puts it on God. Praying in faith also means that we shift the responsibility of the outcome from ourselves to God because we believe He has the answer. He is always good, and His answers to our prayers always result in the best outcome.

Living from a position of fear can bring about disastrous consequences. Fear robs us of the power, peace, and victory we enjoy as God's children, creating false perceptions about our circumstances by making them feel bigger and more daunting. Fear can eradicate hope and become like a poison that infiltrates every aspect of our thinking, slowly killing our peace and position in Christ and leaving us feeling distant from God. God does not intend for us to live in hopelessness or discouragement, nor does He intend for us to intercede from a place devoid of hope. Intercessors cannot afford to live or pray from a position of fear. Often, we must be the ones to hold on to faith when everyone else has succumbed to fear.

Satan's Favorite Weapon

Why is fear such a prominent weapon of the enemy? Because fear takes away our God-given power and allows Satan to control our situation. As a pastor who often served in inner healing and deliverance ministry, I have concluded that fear is Satan's favorite weapon to use against Christians. The devil knows that fear prevents us from living in the fullness of our identity and authority as believers. Without authority, we cannot withstand Satan's attacks because he has the advantage. He uses fear, coupled with lies, to steal, kill, and destroy whatever he can (John 10:10). Satan's aim is to render the Christian powerless and ineffective in both the earthly and spiritual realms. Living from a position of fear robs us of our adoption as children of God and makes us feel like spiritual orphans, always in a state of insecurity and lack. Our freedom, power, and authority collapse under the lies of fear, leaving us in a worse state of mind than an unbeliever.

There should not be any fear in our relationship with God. When we are operating from fear, we are not in alignment with God, Who relates to us in perfect, unlimited love. Love and fear are spiritual opposites. Like oil and water, they do not mix. It was faith in Jesus Christ that brought us into our relationship with God, and it is faith that empowers our lives as Christians. Writing to Timothy, Paul reminds us that God does not bring fear into our lives: *"For the Spirit God gave us does not make us timid, but gives us power, love and self-discipline"* (2 Tim. 1:7). The Passion Translation puts it like this: *"For God will never give you the spirit of fear."*

If we are living our lives or confronting a situation from a spirit of fear, we are not partnering with God—we are partnering with Satan. We are listening to his lies and seeing our world through his colored lenses of fear, which leaves us defeated before we begin to fight.

God-given Power

God has given us power to overcome Satan and every scheme of darkness that perforates our world. 2 Timothy specifically mentions that we have been given power, love, and self-discipline by God. These three elements are important when we are tempted to operate in fear. This power given to us by God is a divine, spiritual power to defeat Satan. As intercessors, we are continually battling dark powers and strategies that want to steal, kill, and destroy whoever and whatever they can. Without power, we cannot face these malicious entities. God is aware that we cannot defeat the forces of darkness in our own strength, so He has equipped us to destroy the works of the enemy through His power. *"For though we live in the world, we do not wage war as the world does. The weapons we fight with are not the weapons of the world. On the contrary, they have divine power to demolish strongholds"* (2 Cor. 10:3-4). We cannot confront the enemy with the power and strength we possess as humans because we are waging war in the spiritual realm (Eph. 6:12). We need spiritual power to defeat spiritual strongholds. God gives us His divine power, which carries the authority to overcome the enemy.

One of the Apostle Paul's prayers for the church at Ephesus details that God has given each Christian, and the church in general, great power that has already overcome the forces of darkness and will continue to defeat Satan when exerted by those who know Him intimately.

> *I keep asking that the God of our Lord Jesus Christ, the glorious Father, may give you the Spirit of wisdom and revelation, so that you may know him better. I pray that the eyes of your heart may be enlightened in order that you may know the hope to which he has called you, the riches of his glorious inheritance in his holy people, and his incomparably **great power for us who believe**. That power is the same as the mighty strength he exerted when he raised Christ from the dead and seated him at his right hand in the heavenly realms, far above all rule and authority, power and dominion, and every name that is invoked, not only in the present age but also in the one to come. And God placed all things under his feet and appointed him to be head over everything for the church, which is his body, the fullness of him who fills everything in every way.*
>
> — EPHESIANS 1:17-23 (EMPHASIS MINE)

This "incomparably great power" we are given is part of our inheritance as sons and daughters of God. It is the same power that was able to raise Christ from the dead and defeat the powers of sin and death in the world, and we have access to it when we pray in faith. It is available to those who know God and, in all faith, believe. Despite such great power at our disposal, many Christians cower at the threats and lies of the enemy when faced with adversity. As intercessors, we have free access to God's armory to fire weapons of prayer against the enemy that will destroy his strongholds and displace his areas of authority.

The church is not only a place of worship. It is also a place of warfare that pushes back the kingdom of darkness and extends God's kingdom of light into the world using spiritual weapons to fight spiritual battles (Eph. 6:10-18). Intercessors are front-line soldiers in spiritual warfare. Prayer is a spiritual act of warfare because it connects us to God's spiritual power to release His will into the earthly realm, defeating the darkness that operates there. In the same way that a battlefield commander radios his headquarters to launch an aerial bombing on an enemy's position, intercession releases God's power and authority against the enemy.

God's Love

In addition to power, God has also given us love. Though we may try to comprehend or explain the depth, width, and volume of God's love, we cannot because God's love is indescribable. Humankind is not intellectually equipped to be able to understand the love of God fully. It is more than our finite minds can grasp. However, we can *experience* His love fully. In fact, we know His love from the very beginning of our conception. As the first cells of our existence begin to split and grow, God's loving hand orchestrates every aspect of our being (Ps. 139:14) and continues as we grow until the time it becomes complete when we receive Jesus into our hearts through salvation. When we repent of our sins and submit ourselves to God through salvation, we experience the fullness of His love as He forgives our sins and adopts us into His family, giving us His Spirit as a deposit of what is to come in eternity. The Holy Spirit enables us to connect with God, to experience His love, and to operate in our inheritance before we enter eternity.

This is how we know that we live in him and he in us: He has given us of his Spirit. And we have seen and testify that the Father has sent his Son to be the Savior of the world. If anyone acknowledges that Jesus is the Son of God, God lives in them and they in God. And so we know and rely on the love God has for us. God is love. Whoever lives in love lives in God, and God in them. This is how love is made complete among us so that we will have confidence on the day of judgment: In this world we are like Jesus. There is no fear in love. But perfect love drives out fear because fear has to do with punishment. The one who fears is not made perfect in love.

— 1 JOHN 4:13-18

We are meant to live in and through God's love. It surrounds and saturates us and gives us the promise of eternity in God's manifest presence when our earthly lives conclude. God's perfect love insulates us from fear. As 1 John states, *"There is no fear in love."* When we truly know and experience God's love, we will not live fearfully. God's love empowers us to reject the lies of the enemy that are intended to create fear. As we come to know and experience His love, we live with assurance that our sins are completely and totally forgiven. We no longer fear God's judgment because the blood of Jesus has washed us clean of sin, taking away the consequences and ability of sin to hold us captive (Isa. 1:18, 1 John 1:7, 9). It is only when we choose to partner with fear that we enter back into spiritual captivity. The enemy works diligently to sow lies in the minds of those who live in God's love because he knows that fear gives him authority and influence over us. If we believe his lies, it is like going to prison for a crime we didn't commit. No one would intentionally do this in an earthly sense, yet we often let Satan's lies spiritually hold us captive through fear.

When we know God's love, we no longer fear punishment for sin. This knowledge brings us spiritual freedom (Gal. 5:1). However, spiritual freedom does not mean we are able to do whatever we desire to do. We still have the boundaries of God's commands to hedge us in. Like the banks of a mighty river, God has given us boundaries that allow us to maintain our spiritual freedom and live in His blessings. *"If* you keep My commandments, you will abide in My love, just as I have kept My Father's commandments and abide in His love"* (John 15:10 NKJV). When we remain within those boundaries we remain in God's love and the enemy cannot infiltrate our life with fear. Fear can only exist where there is an absence of love. We have authority over fear because the light of God's love within us displaces and removes the darkness of fear.

Self-control and Spiritual Discipline

Finally, God has also given us self-control, which is the ability to control our thinking and beliefs to make righteous decisions. The New King James Version of 2 Timothy 1:7 uses the phrase *"a sound mind"* to express what self-control looks like. Our thinking is particularly important when faced with fear. What we think becomes what we believe, and what we believe dictates how we behave. The enemy attacks us primarily with two strategies—fear and lies. Both tactics attack our mind through what we think and what we believe. He wants to plant thoughts of doubt in our minds that will make us question our beliefs, which is how he convinced Adam and Eve to eat of the fruit of the tree of knowledge. Satan caused Eve to doubt God's rules about the tree, making her feel like she was missing out on something she deserved. He is crafty and uses simple lies to make us question God's goodness and promises. Therefore, we must be grounded in God's Word and hold fast to His promises so we are able to discern between the truth and Satan's lies. *"If you hold to my teaching, you are really my disciples. Then you will know the truth, and the truth will set you free"* (John 8:31-32).

God is aware of Satan's strategies, which is why He has given us power, love, and a sound mind to combat fear. Therefore, we must submit our mind to Christ (1 Cor. 2:16) because when we do, we can apply the power we carry and remain in God's love. To do this, our thoughts and beliefs must be grounded in faith. Do you genuinely believe that God is good? Do you believe that your sins have been forgiven? Do you believe that God is your provider and protector? Do you believe that God can overcome whatever situation you are facing? These are simple questions, but many Christians' actions demonstrate that they do not believe in God's power and character to sustain their lives. Although we may say we believe, our actions ultimately reveal what is in our heart. The greatest question we must ask is, "Who am I believing?" If your answer is "Satan," you will live from a position of fear. If it is "God," you will live from a position of faith.

I spoke earlier of the contrast between our earthly and spiritual realities. Satan focuses on our earthly reality to create doubt and fear in our thinking. He knows that we will become fearful if we live from this viewpoint. The blood of Jesus has cleansed us from all unrighteousness and sin, yet we are very aware our sinful nature still exists (1 John 1:9). Satan likes to remind us of the things we have done wrong.

He wants us to focus on our sin and the shame it brings. This is an earthly reality. The spiritual reality is that we are holy before God. We are now seated with Christ in heavenly places. We cannot be in God's presence if we are still full of sin and unrighteousness. Ephesians 2 clearly explains how our earthly reality is superseded by our spiritual reality when we become Christians.

As for you, you were dead in your transgressions and sins, in which you used to live when you followed the ways of this world and of the ruler of the kingdom of the air, the spirit who is now at work in those who are disobedient. All of us also lived among them at one time, gratifying the cravings of our flesh and following its desires and thoughts. Like the rest, we were by nature deserving of wrath. But because of his great love for us, God, who is rich in mercy, made us alive with Christ even when we were dead in transgressions—it is by grace you have been saved. And God raised us up with Christ and seated us with him in the heavenly realms in Christ Jesus, in order that in the coming ages he might show the incomparable riches of his grace, expressed in his kindness to us in Christ Jesus. For it is by grace you have been saved, through faith—and this is not from yourselves, it is the gift of God—not by works, so that no one can boast.

— EPHESIANS 2:1-9

According to Ephesians 2, we are seated with Christ in the heavenly realms. This is our spiritual reality. Satan wants us to continue living in our old earthly reality of sin, judgment, and death, and uses lies to make us doubt our identity and position with Christ. When we believe that we are made holy through Jesus, it changes how we live. We must not let the accusations of shame and guilt that the enemy hurls at us penetrate our thinking. Instead, we must continually align our thinking with God's truth. *"Do not conform to the pattern of this world, but be transformed by the renewing of your mind. Then you will be able to test and approve what God's will is —his good, pleasing and perfect will"* (Rom. 12:2).

It is our faith in our position in Christ and God's character that will deflect the fiery arrows of the enemy (Eph. 6:16). Applied faith overcomes fear because we choose to believe what God says about us instead of what we perceive or experience in our earthly existence. If we believe that we are holy, we will most likely behave in a holy manner. If we believe that our sin still covers us with shame and guilt, we will most likely behave accordingly because we feel unworthy, powerless, and tainted. We become afraid to confront the enemy because we feel inadequate to overcome his schemes. This kind of thinking will keep us from stepping into our spiritual gifts, leaving a gap in our church.

Fear is a powerful force, but it is easily avoided or overcome when we focus on the truth and reject the enemy's lies. *"You will keep in perfect peace those whose minds are steadfast, because they trust in you"* (Isa. 26:3). A sound mind remains at peace regardless of what our earthly eyes see. God's love, power, and truth have been given to us so we do not have to live as captives to fear. As intercessors, we need to know God's will so we can agree and proclaim it through our intercession, praying in faith and seeing God respond in incredible ways. To do this means we must daily renew our minds so we can pray with power. A sound mind founded on our experience of God's love and truth produces faith that overcomes all fear. This is self-control. God has given us everything we need to live a life of powerful faith. Choosing to live by either faith or fear carries significant implications and outcomes. Faith is the weapon we must use against the enemy and our source of hope when we pray.

6

THE PRINCIPLES OF CONTENDING PRAYER AND FASTING

As a child, did you ever desire a toy so much that you begged your parents relentlessly for it? Did you get it? As a parent, I know how it is to have a child continue to pester me for something they want. My son focuses in and will diligently ask for it until he either gets it or realizes that it is definitely not going to happen. He is persistent. His persistence is a quality that I hope will mature and become an asset for him as an adult.

God is often called our Father, and we are called His children. We have a familial relationship with God by our spiritual adoption through salvation. He wants us to bring our requests to Him, although sometimes, we must ask often and consistently. While God loves to bless us, His children, there are times when we don't see our prayers answered immediately. That does not necessarily mean the answer is "no." We have all probably heard testimonies of a mother faithfully praying for a child to come to the Lord. Sometimes it takes many years to happen, but that mother never gives up in her faithful prayers. I personally know mothers who have not yet seen their prayers answered, but they continue to ask God to intervene in their children's lives, believing that He is working despite the way the situation appears. This is called contending prayer.

Contending prayer is a type of intercession that is focused and persistent and often comes from a place of great need or discomfort. Usually, a burden or problem becomes the catalyst for a season of contending prayer. When we contend in prayer, we refuse to relent as long as the situation persists. This does not mean that God will give us whatever we want simply because we pester Him long enough. We do not contend for selfish needs or desires. We use the practice of contending prayer when we are faced with a situation that only God's power and justice can address. Scripture says when we pray in line with God's will, He will answer. However, there are times when persistent prayer is required to achieve a righteous outcome.

Contending prayer can be a powerful form of praying because we are conducting a spiritual battle between God's will and current circumstances that are *not* in alignment with His will. Those engaged in contending prayer push through the discomfort of the waiting and disappointment by staying focused on seeing their prayers answered because they believe God is faithful to His word. They pray with great faith, believing that God is the only one Who can answer their prayers and change the situation. These types of prayers are not focused on asking God for basic needs as we might do in our daily prayers. In contrast, contending prayer tends to deal with serious, miraculous matters that can only be fulfilled by God. Things like revival, the return of a wayward child, and injustice are the sorts of things that stir a person or group to contend in prayer.

The best biblical example of contending prayer comes from Luke 18. This passage starts by stating, *"Then Jesus told his disciples a parable to show them that they should always pray and not give up"* (Luke 18:1). I think it is important to note that Jesus is teaching His disciples that persistent, continual prayer is part of their responsibility as His followers. He is encouraging them to *"pray without ceasing"* (1 Thess. 5:17 NKJV). When our earthly circumstances do not reflect our spiritual reality, we must learn to pray and contend for a change. Because the act of contending prayer is introduced to us by Jesus Himself, it is something that every intercessor should pay attention to and understand. Jesus goes on to use a parable to demonstrate how contending prayer should operate.

He said: "In a certain town there was a judge who neither feared God nor cared what people thought. And there was a widow in that town who kept coming to him with the plea, 'Grant me justice against my adversary.' "For some time he refused. But finally he said to himself, 'Even though I don't fear God or care what people think, yet because this widow keeps bothering me, I will see that she gets justice, so that she won't eventually come and attack me!'" And the Lord said, "Listen to what the unjust judge says. And will not God bring about justice for his chosen ones, who cry out to him day and night? Will he keep putting them off? I tell you, he will see that they get justice, and quickly. However, when the Son of Man comes, will he find faith on the earth?"

— LUKE 18:2-8

A Plea for Justice

Although this parable from Luke is a short one, it is full of principles that demonstrate how we should contend in prayer. First, the widow is petitioning for justice against her adversary. She has a situation in which justice has been denied her. This is a vital detail. When the topic of our contending prayer is seeking justice, I believe God listens and responds. We do not know the details of her situation, but whatever it is, she is not going to rest until she has resolution. God is a just God. He does not take injustice lightly. Psalm 11:7 tells us, *"For the Lord is righteous, he loves justice; the upright will see his face."* Injustice comes in many forms. We experience injustice when we are either denied what we deserve or have been given something we do not deserve. Contending prayer petitions God for what He has promised us through His Word. When sin or the decisions of others deny us of those promises, we have the authority to contend in prayer to God to see those promises fulfilled.

God Loves Justice

The next principle of contending prayer in Luke 18 is that God loves justice. What a fortunate dynamic; we need justice and God loves to see justice done. That is what I call a win-win situation. God will not withhold justice from His children. Jesus points out that even an unjust judge will release justice when petitioned continually. If an unjust judge will give justice, how much more will God, our Righteous Judge, see to it that we receive justice? Jesus goes on to say that God will give us justice in a quick time frame. We must remember that His time frame is vastly different to ours. Sometimes we can pray one day and find resolution the next. However, there are times when "quickly" may mean years. God works outside of the confines of our time, which is why contending prayer is a vital discipline to develop as an intercessor (2 Peter 3:8). Here are a few scriptures that speak of the justice of God:

"The LORD is known by his acts of justice; the wicked are ensnared by the work of their hands" (Psalm 9:16).

"The LORD loves righteousness and justice; the earth is full of his unfailing love" (Psalm 33:5).

"Your righteousness is like the highest mountains, your justice like the great deep. You, LORD, preserve both people and animals" (Psalm 36:6).

"Your throne, O God, will last for ever and ever; a scepter of justice will be the scepter of your kingdom" (Psalm 45:6).

"And the heavens proclaim his righteousness, for he is a God of justice" (Psalm 50:6).

"Righteousness and justice are the foundation of your throne; love and faithfulness go before you" (Psalm 89:14).

"The LORD works righteousness and justice for all the oppressed" (Psalm 103:6).

"Many seek an audience with a ruler, but it is from the LORD that one gets justice" (Proverbs 29:26).

"But the LORD Almighty will be exalted by his justice, and the holy God will be proved holy by his righteous acts" (Isaiah 5:16).

"Here is my servant whom I have chosen, the one I love, in whom I delight; I will put my Spirit on him, and he will proclaim justice to the nations" (Matthew 12:18).

IN MANY OF THESE VERSES, God's character is described as righteous and just. You might say that justice is in His DNA and is as much a part of His character as love and holiness. I am focusing on this part of His character because when we are contending in prayer over a matter of injustice, it stirs God's heart and He will respond to us, His children. *"Yet the LORD longs to be gracious to you; therefore he will rise up to show you compassion. For the LORD is a God of justice. Blessed are all who wait for him"* (Isa. 30:18)! Our pleas do not fall on deaf ears. God is moved by His love for us according to His just character. Although we may not see or perceive it for a time, God is always working (Ps. 121:4). Contending prayer believes in faith that God is working despite what we see and experience in the meantime. One of the differences between contending prayer and normal prayer is that when we contend, we continue to pray until the situation is resolved and our prayers are answered.

Contending Prayer Requires Determination and Consistency

The third principle we learn from this parable is that contending prayer is not a one-off type of praying. It requires determination and consistency. The widow "kept coming" to the unjust judge with her plea. Jesus does not tell us how many times she petitioned this judge, but it was enough that he realized she was not going to relent in pleading her case. She was so persistent that she became a nuisance to the judge. Her constant pleas bothered him. He gave in and gave her justice so that she would stop pestering him. When we contend in prayer to God, we are not pleading with an unjust judge. We are petitioning our loving Father, Who is compassionate toward our situation. It is our faith in God's character that sustains us to continue to press in. We must believe that He is just and will answer our prayers and then be disciplined to continue to pray as we wait on the resolution. This kind of persistence requires faith and intentionality.

A Prodigal Returns

I recently heard the testimony of a pastor in the United States named Karen Wheaton that demonstrates God's faithfulness regarding contending prayer. Her youngest daughter, Lindsey, was raised in church, married to a pastor, and serving in ministry when she suddenly decided to leave her husband and live a different life. This was devastating for everyone involved. Although her heart was broken, Karen refused to accept this situation as God's plan for Lindsey's life. A righteous indignation arose in her spirit. She began to contend in prayer for Lindsey. As she prayed, God would respond with words of encouragement from the Bible and with prophetic revelation. Karen would take these words and use them to contend for Lindsey's life and marriage to be restored. She would pray these scriptures out loud and prophetically declare that Lindsey would return to what she knew was right. One of the verses the Lord gave Karen is from Isaiah:

Can plunder be taken from warriors, or captives be rescued from the fierce? But this is what the LORD says: "Yes, captives will be taken from warriors, and plunder retrieved from the fierce; I will contend with those who contend with you, and your children I will save.

— ISAIAH 49:24-25

It was scripture like this that sustained Karen to continue to seek God in prayer. The whole situation lasted for two years. It was not resolved immediately, but Karen continued to pray, and God kept His promises to her. After two years, Lindsey did return home and was able to rescue her marriage. Thankfully, the final signature needed to make her divorce official had not been signed by the judge. Lindsey and her husband reunited, and she has been restored to ministry, her family, and to God. Praise God for His faithfulness and grace! (Used with permission).

In my own life, I have seen the power of contending prayer. I am an American married to an Australian. When we first got married, we began our life together in the United States. Bronwen had just finished her university studies and I had a job as a youth pastor at a small church outside Atlanta. We lived in Atlanta for the first six years of our marriage before moving to Brisbane, Australia. While we were dating, I visited Australia for the first time and went to the church that Bronwen attended while she was a student. Kenmore Baptist Church was a vibrant and exciting church with many young people and a passionate pastoral leadership team. During the service, I nudged Bronwen and half-jokingly said that maybe I could serve at this church if we moved to Australia in the future. She laughed and said it would never happen because most of the pastoral team were related by blood or marriage. At the time, her observation was true. Most of the staff were related! I ignored her negativity and secretly filed the idea away in the back of my mind. This was 1999.

Fast forward to the end of 2006, and we had just moved to Australia. I had agreed to move with a great deal of reluctance because it meant leaving behind my family, ministry, and all the familiarities of home. Bronwen was working for the Australian government and was transferred to Australia to take on a new role. I wanted to support her career and maintain my marriage, so I chose to pack up and move to Brisbane. The first few months were quite difficult, as I did not know anyone. I was in an unfamiliar country I had only briefly visited twice before, living with my in-laws on the Gold Coast while Bronwen worked in Sydney (about 1000 kms south of the Gold Coast). Bronwen's parents did not really know me, and I did not know them. Bronwen and I dated for two years before we got married, but most of that time it was long-distance, as she lived in Brisbane and I lived in Atlanta. There were certainly awkward moments as I got to know my Australian family without the buffer of my wife to make it easier, but we all tried our best to make the situation as smooth as possible.

When we arrived in Australia, I did not have a job and did not have any viable ministry contacts to help me find one. At least, I didn't *think* I had the right contacts. It is common to use networking to find a new pastoral role. Usually, you know someone who knows someone, and the connection is made. The only pastor I had any connection with was Pastor John Robertson from Kenmore Baptist Church who had conducted our wedding six years earlier. I had only met John on the day of our wedding and did not engage with him very much outside of the formalities of the ceremony. I decided to muster up some courage and give John a call. I began by sharing that I had recently moved to Brisbane and was looking for a pastoral role. Thankfully, John remembered me because Bronwen had been so active in the church during her university years. We set a date to meet. Over lunch, John revealed that Kenmore Baptist was currently looking for a new young adult pastor. Our conversation increasingly took the tone of a job interview, and before it was over, he asked me to send him my resume, as he thought the job might be a good fit for both of us.

I came away shocked at the way God had orchestrated the whole series of events. After several official interviews, I was offered the position and began working at Kenmore Baptist Church in March 2007. I was so excited to have found a new role with an amazing church. Unbeknownst to me was the fact that Bronwen's mother had been consistently praying that I would get a pastoral role at Kenmore Baptist the entire time we were living in America. She had contended in prayer for nearly six years. I believe it was the power of her prayers that motivated God to bring all these puzzle pieces together.

Eventually, Kenmore Baptist grew and moved. As part of the move, they changed the name to Riverlife Baptist Church. I served on staff for fourteen years at Riverlife. As I have mentioned before, the journey of this church and my own personal journey have run parallel in my understanding and experience of the Holy Spirit. It was at Riverlife that I experienced the empowerment of the Holy Spirit and learned how to lead intercessors effectively. I am thankful that my mother-in-law secretly contended in prayer for me all those years. My life has been immeasurably blessed by the results of her prayers.

Contending through Disappointment

One of the differences between contending prayer and normal intercession is the duration that is required for contending prayer. Many times, an intercessor must continue to pray about the situation for many weeks, months, or years. There will be times when the situation may likely get worse before it gets better. Those engaged in contending prayer must see setbacks as motivation to press in more passionately. It is important not to give up, but to hang on to the promises of God and keep praying. Contending prayer can sometimes be a form of spiritual warfare against the devil. Those contending in prayer defiantly stand against the works of the enemy and declare God's will and promises over the situation. Praying God's will is a strategy that will bring us the victory if we do not give up. *"This is the confidence we have in approaching God: that if we ask anything according to his will, he hears us. And if we know that he hears us—whatever we ask—we know that we have what we asked of him"* (1 John 5:14-15).

When we are contending in prayer for God's will, whatever we ask for will be done. This is an incredible promise that requires faith to see our requests come to fruition. Faith is the food that sustains an intercessor contending in prayer. When the situation gets worse instead of better as we pray, our faith must be engaged to remain hopeful and continue to persevere. Faith is the key. Jesus encourages us, *"If you believe, you will receive whatever you ask for in prayer"* (Matt. 21:22).

"Have faith in God," Jesus answered. "Truly I tell you, if anyone says to this mountain, 'Go, throw yourself into the sea,' and does not doubt in their heart but believes that what they say will happen, it will be done for them. Therefore, I tell you, whatever you ask for in prayer, believe that you have received it, and it will be yours.

— MARK 11:22-24

Contending with Others

Although we can individually contend in prayer, it can be more effective if we recruit others to contend with us. As has been discussed earlier, agreement in prayer by two or more people engages the presence of Jesus with those praying (Matt. 18:19-20). Contending in prayer with others also gives us confidence and support. We will not feel alone in the situation and will be strengthened by the support of other intercessors praying in cooperation with us. Contending in prayer with others also helps us carry the load of the burden we are praying for, especially if the outcome is delayed. The support of trusted friends and family standing with us gives us strength when we are tired and need someone to take the load for a while. When we pray with others, we are also multiplying our ability to hear from God. 1 Corinthians 13:9 reminds us that *we know in part and we prophesy in part."* Each intercessor can bring their part of the picture, which helps us to know how to continue praying more clearly.

One of my favorite Bible stories demonstrates the power of contending in prayer with others. As a young man, Daniel had been taken from his family in Judah and put into service for King Nebuchadnezzar in Babylon. King Nebuchadnezzar did not worship God, and the environment that Daniel and the other young Israelites faced was hostile toward their faith. Despite this challenging situation, Daniel faithfully served several evil kings during his life, often bringing glory to God. Daniel's life and service to these kings are incredible examples of how to faithfully intercede when faced with great trials.

At some point, King Nebuchadnezzar had a dream that

disturbed him, so he called in his wise men to interpret it for him. The only problem was that the king would not tell the wise men what he saw in his dream. Instead, the king demanded that they describe the nature of his dream and the interpretation. He wanted to test them to make sure they were not just telling him what they thought he wanted to hear. Those wise men, who were magicians, enchanters, sorcerers, and astrologers protested the king's request because they knew they could not tell him the nature of his dream and interpret it. King Nebuchadnezzar doubled down and replied,

---

This is what I have firmly decided: If you do not tell me what my dream was and interpret it, I will have you cut into pieces and your houses turned into piles of rubble. But if you tell me the dream and explain it, you will receive from me gifts and rewards and great honor. So, tell me the dream and interpret it for me.

— DANIEL 2:5-6

Again, the wise men protested, "There is no one on earth who can do what the king asks! No king, however great and mighty, has ever asked such a thing of any magician or enchanter or astrologer. What the king asks is too difficult. No one can reveal *it to the king except the gods, and they do not live among humans"* (Dan. 2:10-11). This made King Nebuchadnezzar extremely angry. He wanted answers, not excuses. In his frustration, he decreed that all the wise men of Babylon be executed. This included Daniel and his exiled companions.

To enforce this decree, King Nebuchadnezzar sent out his royal guard to collect all the wise men of Babylon that they might be killed. When Arioch, the commander of the king's guard, found Daniel, he told Daniel of the king's decree. Daniel asked why the king had issued such a harsh command, and upon learning of the king's unreasonable request, Daniel bravely decided to go before the king to ask for more time, promising that he would interpret the dream. The king agreed, and Daniel recruited some friends to contend with him in prayer for the dream and its interpretation.

Then Daniel returned to his house and explained the matter to his friends Hananiah, Mishael, and Azariah. He urged them to plead for mercy from the God of heaven concerning this mystery, so that he and his friends might not be executed with the rest of the wise men of Babylon. During the night the mystery was revealed to Daniel in a vision. Then Daniel praised the God of heaven.

— DANIEL 2:17-19

The next morning, Daniel went to Arioch and asked him to take him to the king so that he might reveal the dream and its interpretation to save himself and the other wise men of Babylon from being executed. As Daniel stood before King Nebuchadnezzar, he began his speech by declaring that *"No wise man, enchanter, magician or diviner can explain to the king the mystery he has asked about, but there is a God in heaven who reveals mysteries"* (Dan. 2:27-28a). Daniel did not take credit for what he was about to share with the king, but gave God the glory.

Like Daniel, intercessors should always give God the glory for the answers and direction they receive from Him. When we receive prophetic revelation, we should thank God and praise Him before doing anything else. As Daniel revealed the dream and gave the interpretation, King Nebuchadnezzar was overwhelmed and fell to his face before Daniel, declaring, *"Surely your God is the God of gods and the Lord of kings and a revealer of mysteries, for you were able to reveal this mystery"* (Dan. 2:47).

When faced with the possibility of being executed along with all the other wise men in Babylon, Daniel did what a wise intercessor should do—he contended in prayer to the Lord and the Lord answered him, which enabled Daniel to tell the king his dream and give an accurate interpretation. Daniel's recollection and interpretation of the king's dream saved all the wise men and gave glory to God. For a moment, even King Nebuchadnezzar acknowledged God's glory and gave Him praise. Notice that Daniel did not take on this challenge alone. Although it was Daniel who received the vision, he was supported by his three friends as they contended in prayer. I believe the revelation came as quickly as it did because Daniel and his friends agreed in prayer.

Daniel is a dynamic character in the Bible, and his life is worth studying if you are called to intercession. The testimonies of God's faithfulness to answer Daniel's prayers are throughout the book of Daniel, where he is often found contending in prayer. In each instance, God released the prophetic revelation that Daniel and other intercessors needed because of their persistence and faithfulness.

The Spiritual Discipline of Fasting

Fasting is one of the most powerful spiritual disciplines we can participate in as Christian intercessors. As such, fasting and contending prayer are commonly exercised together. Whatever the situation is that motivates us to contend in prayer, the discipline of fasting increases our time and focus to pray. As we deny ourselves of something important and dedicate that time to prayer and being in God's presence, it transforms us from within. Our inner transformation can then make an impact in our sphere of influence.

Most people think that fasting is the denial of food for a designated time, and although fasting from food is probably the most common form of fasting, we can also fast from other things that are taking our time and attention away from God and see similar results. Fasting is always transformative because we intentionally increase the time we spend with the Lord. When we are in His presence, we cannot help but be changed. Moses' encounter with the Lord at Mt. Sinai and in the tent of meeting are documented examples that being in God's presence is transformative.

When Moses came down from Mount Sinai with the two tablets of the covenant law in his hands, he was not aware that his face was radiant because he had spoken with the LORD. When Aaron and all the Israelites saw Moses, his face was radiant, and they were afraid to come near him. But Moses called to them; so Aaron and all the leaders of the community came back to him, and he spoke to them. Afterward all the Israelites came near him, and he gave them all the commands the LORD had given him on Mount Sinai. When Moses finished speaking to them, he put a veil over his face. But whenever he entered the LORD's presence to speak with him, he removed the veil until he came out. And when he came out and told the Israelites what he had been commanded, they saw that his face was radiant. Then Moses would put the veil back over his face until he went in to speak with the LORD.

— EXODUS 34:29-35

We may not glow as Moses did from spending time in God's presence, but we will be different for it.

Fasting helps us listen to God's voice because it eliminates the distractions of our normal routine as we set aside things like meals so we can focus on what God is saying and doing in us. It is an important spiritual discipline because it sharpens our ability to wait on God and listen to what He is saying, which is essentially the job of an intercessor. Metaphorically, fasting is an intensive workshop on intercession, teaching us to tune in to God's voice clearly. This helps us to recognize and hear God's voice in times when we are not fasting as well. We fast, contend in prayer, wait on the Lord, listen to what He is saying, and then declare His will through our prayers.

In a later chapter in the book of Daniel, we see Daniel fasting as he contended in prayer. Daniel had received a vision of a great war that was coming and was deeply moved by what he had seen. From the day he received the vision, Daniel fasted and contended in prayer. Scripture tells us that God heard his prayers and sent a messenger to answer him, but the messenger was delayed, so Daniel continued to pray and fast for three weeks. Eventually, the messenger reached Daniel and explained the situation.

> *He said, "Daniel, you who are highly esteemed, consider carefully the words I am about to speak to you, and stand up, for I have now been sent to you." And when he said this to me, I stood up trembling. Then he continued, "Do not be afraid, Daniel. Since the first day that you set your mind to gain understanding and to humble yourself before your God, your words were heard, and I have come in response to them. But the prince of the Persian kingdom resisted me twenty-one days. Then Michael, one of the chief princes, came to help me, because I was detained there with the king of Persia. Now I have come to explain to you what will happen to your people in the future, for the vision concerns a time yet to come."*
>
> — DANIEL 10:11-14

It is interesting to note that the answer to Daniel's prayers was delayed by the "prince of Persia." Most scholars believe that this was not an earthly prince, but a spiritual prince or territorial spirit. This prince would probably fall under the category of rulers, authorities, or spiritual forces of evil in the heavenly realms that Paul mentions in Ephesians 6:12. We do not know where this prince stood within the spiritual hierarchy of authority, but it is reasonable to assume that he was powerful if he was able to delay God's messenger for three weeks. Often, our prayers are in direct opposition to the spiritual authorities operating in the world, engaging us in a spiritual battle between God's will and our current circumstances. The faithful persistence of contending prayer continues to seek God's will being done despite the delayed outcome.

Love Is Our Motivation

Although he was still in exile, Daniel's heart was full of compassion for his homeland and his people. Love was his motivation to contend in prayer for their well-being after seeing a vision predicting war. Love must always be the foundational motivation to intercede for others. Daniel was willing to deny himself of food and comfort to devote his time to praying for his people out of love.

Once God's messenger was able to overcome the prince of Persia, he went on to explain in detail what would occur in the future, even going so far as to mention the end times. The messenger finished his time with Daniel by encouraging him, *"As for you, go your way till the end. You will rest, and then at the end of the days you will rise to receive your allotted inheritance"* (Dan. 12:13).

Another biblical example of fasting and contending prayer comes from Deuteronomy 9. The rebellious and "stiff-necked people" of Israel were always arousing God's anger. Thus, Moses often served as a buffer between the Israelites and God's impending judgment. In this instance, the Israelites are about to cross over into the land God had promised them. Moses reminded them that this blessing was not due to their righteousness, but because of the wickedness of the cities in the land. He told them that he had to fast and contend in prayer with the Lord for forty days and nights to turn away God's wrath toward them. Moses declared, *"I feared the anger and wrath of the LORD, for he was angry enough with you to destroy you. But again, the LORD listened to me"* (Deut. 9:19).

Moses knew the righteousness of God and that His standard was holiness. This was a man who had on numerous occasions spoken to God face-to-face as a man would do with his friend (Exod. 33:11). Moses knew God's character better than any other man. When he saw the people worshipping the idol of Baal, he knew that God's righteous wrath would be aroused significantly. In response, Moses fasted and prayed, pleading with God to turn His wrath away. In verses 25-29, he recounts what happened:

I lay prostrate before the LORD those forty days and forty nights because the LORD had said he would destroy you. I prayed to the LORD and said, "Sovereign LORD, do not destroy your people, your own inheritance that you redeemed by your great power and brought out of Egypt with a mighty hand. Remember

> *your servants Abraham, Isaac and Jacob. Overlook the stubbornness of this people, their wickedness and their sin. Otherwise, the country from which you brought us will say, 'Because the LORD was not able to take them into the land he had promised them, and because he hated them, he brought them out to put them to death in the wilderness.' But they are your people, your inheritance that you brought out by your great power and your outstretched arm."*
>
> — DEUTERONOMY 9:25-29

In this case, the duration of contending prayer was dictated by how long Moses fasted. The situation was quite serious, causing Moses to sacrifice his food and drink on behalf of the nation. Although the scripture does not specifically address it, I can only imagine that it was Moses' love for his people that motivated him to fast and pray on their behalf. God's wrath was turned away, as He did not destroy the Israelites.

Fasting as we contend in prayer can make our requests to God more intense and focused. Obviously, if you are fasting from food, you cannot do so indefinitely. However, this does not mean that you must stop praying when the fast is over. As intercessors, we will be faced with circumstances that require us to consistently pray and not become discouraged by what seems impossible by our earthly perceptions and understanding, believing in faith that God can overcome whatever we are facing. Remember, contending prayer stands in opposition to our earthly circumstances and the work of the enemy to bring God's will to fruition.

Yet, contending prayer does not always have to be open-ended. There are times when we contend for a predetermined time, and if we fast in conjunction with contending prayer, the time frame may be limited. Fasting allows us to intentionally enter God's presence more often, especially when the circumstances are dire. Waiting on God to reveal His will is a key element. It is good to write down what you hear God saying, whether it be prophetic revelation or a scripture verse, and pray in agreement with His promises and His will. Together, contending prayer and fasting are two powerful weapons for intercessors to wield as we pray for those we love and serve.

7
PROPHETIC SYMBOLISM IN INTERCESSION

By nature, I am deeply introverted. I do not dance. I prefer doing most of my hobbies and leisure activities alone as opposed to those who participate in activities for the social aspect. For instance, I enjoy mountain biking by myself. It allows me to experience nature's beauty on my own, I don't have to talk to anyone, and I can go at my own pace. It has been challenging at times to break out of my introversion and be obedient to what God wants so a breakthrough can occur, especially in my role as leader of an intercessory prayer team. There have been many times when God has led the intercessors to cooperate with His will through a prophetic action that was outside of my introverted comfort zone. Typically, it is the extroverts of the team who push me to engage in some form of prophetic gesture. I am thankful for their willingness to embarrass themselves for the sake of being obedient to God. They drag me with them, and honestly, it has often been fun.

Before we go any further, I want to define what I mean by "prophetic gestures" or "prophetic symbolism". Simply put, these terms are my attempt to describe what sometimes happens during intercession. A prophetic gesture is a physical action or activity that has spiritual meaning. It is meant to demonstrate in the natural what is happening spiritually. It is prophetic because the source of these gestures originates from God and is usually given through a word of knowledge. A common prophetic gesture in the Bible is the pouring of oil over a person. The oil is symbolic of the Holy Spirit's presence and anointing. It can also represent consecration to God for His purposes (Exod. 29, Lev. 8). In the New Testament, anointing with oil often symbolizes physical cleansing and brings about physical healing (Mark 6:13, James 5:14-15). There is no supernatural power in the oil. Rather, it is symbolic of God's presence in our earthly realm while He is acting in the spiritual realm, whether it be for healing, consecration, anointing, or some other purpose.

Prophetic Gestures in Intercession

There will be times when interceding that God prompts you to engage in a prophetic gesture—to act in a physical way so as to symbolize what is happening in the spiritual. These prophetic gestures in the earthly realm have impact in the spiritual realm. When I pray with someone who has been involved in witchcraft or Freemasonry, we will often remove spiritual rings, jewelry, or articles of clothing by mimicking the action physically. We cannot physically see the items with our eyes, but that item does exist on the person in the spiritual realm. The result of such prophetic gestures can be powerful and freeing. These sorts of gestures are symbolic and demonstrate our faith that God is working in the spiritual realm in parallel action to our physical actions.

Sometimes a prophetic gesture may be as simple as slashing your arm forward as you declare you are cutting off some spiritual authority that has attached to a person or a situation. Other times, a prophetic gesture might be expressed by flying a prayer flag over a person symbolizing God's love, healing, joy, or a plethora of other things. The prayer flag represents what God is releasing over that person at that time.

You may think this is all a bit too weird and that only fanatical Christians would engage in such behavior. I would caution you from judging the relevancy of prophetic gestures and symbolism too quickly. A fellow pastor I served with once expressed skepticism about the relevancy of prayer flags until he had a powerful experience that changed his perspective. During one of our weekend discipleship retreats, he was overcome in the Spirit and was lying on the ground under the power of God. Someone decided to drape a prayer flag over him that symbolized what God was doing. For three hours, he was unable to get up. The weight of the flag restricted him from moving from where he was. No matter how hard he tried, he was unable to get up. In the natural, it was only a light-weight flag made of a silky material weighing barely an ounce, but the spiritual ministry God was doing within him made the flag supernaturally heavy. He is no longer a skeptic.

One of the most beautiful prophetic gestures of the Bible is the story of Mary anointing Jesus' feet with expensive perfume (John 12:1-8). I am not sure what motivated Mary to perform this prophetic gesture, but it was an extravagant and costly demonstration of her love for Jesus. Some have said the perfume cost the equivalent of a year's wages. This anointing occurred at a dinner with other guests watching Mary's loving act. Some of the guests became offended and suggested that the perfume was wasted and should have been sold so the profits could be given to the poor. Jesus recognized the gesture for what it was and defended Mary's actions. He told the guests that this perfume was meant for His day of burial, knowing that His crucifixion and death would occur a short time later. Mary prepared Jesus for what was coming by performing this beautiful prophetic gesture.

Symbolism in Christian Tradition

Admittedly, prophetic gestures and symbolism can seem a bit strange at times because we are trying to express spiritual realities with our limited earthly bodies. If you are like me, these gestures often feel awkward, uncomfortable, and possibly even silly. This does not discount the power of obediently following God's direction. Many of our most solemn traditions are symbolic in nature. In the Baptist denomination, we baptize new believers by fully immersing them in a tank of water. The act of baptism is symbolic of a spiritual reality. As a result of our salvation, the Bible tells us that we have died to our old, fleshly self just as Christ died on the cross (2 Cor. 5:17). When we enter the baptismal pool, it is representative of the old person dying. As we enter the water completely, we are symbolizing the burial of Jesus. Coming out of the water is symbolic of Jesus' resurrection and our new life that is now in Christ. Water baptism does not save us—it is a symbolic public declaration of what has occurred within us spiritually. We have died to our old life of sin and are now spiritually alive in Jesus. The Apostle Paul describes the spiritual reality that baptism represents eloquently in Galatians 2:20: *"I have been crucified with Christ and I no longer live, but Christ lives in me. The life I now live in the body, I live by faith in the Son of God, who loved me and gave himself for me."*

Communion is another symbolic tradition that represents a greater spiritual reality. Jesus instituted the tradition of communion during the Last Supper with His disciples before He was crucified.

> *While they were eating, Jesus took bread, and when he had given thanks, he broke it and gave it to his disciples, saying, "Take and eat; this is my body." Then he took a cup, and when he had given thanks, he gave it to them, saying, "Drink from it, all of you. This is my blood of the covenant, which is poured out for many for the forgiveness of sins."*
>
> — MATTHEW 26:26-28

In Luke's account of the Last Supper, he includes the phrase, "do this in remembrance of me" (Luke 22:19). Thus, the tradition of communion was established. The bread represents the broken body of Jesus, and the wine represents His blood shed for our sins. Every time we partake in communion, we are symbolically remembering the incredible sacrifice Jesus made on the cross for our sins. The elements of bread and wine are symbolic of Christ's body and blood that was poured out for us.

A Christian wedding also contains symbolic gestures. The wedding ring is a symbol of the vows and promises that each partner is making to the other. It symbolizes their love for one another and serves as a reminder of their commitment, as it is worn on the hand. As it is circular with no end, the love of the couple should be without end. Marriage is a sacred covenant between two people that not only brings physical connection, but also spiritually binds two people together (Gen. 2:24). Brides typically wear a white dress to symbolize their purity entering the relationship.

We all accept this kind of symbolism because we understand the meaning it is conveying. It should be no different in intercession when we engage in prophetically symbolic activities. We should not be afraid of using symbolism in prophetic intercession as long as it has a clear purpose and meaning. There is no reason why we should not take it just as seriously as we do other elements of symbolism in Christianity.

Several years ago, the intercessory prayer team and I were praying for our church when the Lord moved in our hearts, telling us that we should stand in a circle and hold hands. We were praying about the sense of exhaustion and heaviness in our services. We felt like we needed to intercede by rejoicing and dancing. Like a group of children doing the Hokey Pokey, we put our hands in and out and up and down. This created a lot of laughter and joy. As we danced, we shouted our praises to God through the laughter and smiles. I am sure we would have looked ridiculous to any onlooker, but this prophetic gesture released joy into each one of us and into the church atmosphere. It was fun for me despite being outside my comfort zone.

By being willing to do something different in our intercession session, the spiritual atmosphere shifted from heaviness to joy. God loves joy. We do not have to avoid having fun when we intercede because the joy of the Lord is our strength. *"You make known to me the path of life; you will fill me with joy in your presence, with eternal pleasures at your right hand"* (Ps. 16:11). Intercession does not always have to be solemn, serious work. If we are in God's presence, there should be joy. Although the Hokey Pokey prophetic gesture might seem silly, God used it powerfully to restore joy in our Sunday services.

The Battle of Jericho

I believe the story of the battle of Jericho demonstrates how prophetic gestures can be powerful. In this biblical story, the Israelites are beginning to enter the Promised Land and come up against Jericho, the most formidable challenge the nation had faced so far. Jericho was a heavily fortified city with extremely high and thick walls. The city also had food and water rations to withstand an attack for about a year. A normal battle plan would be to surround the city and wait until all the supplies ran out, forcing the inhabitants to emerge to fight. Instead, God told Joshua to march around the city blowing horns and shouting. This must be one of the most unique battle plans in history. From a military perspective, marching around the walls of a city blowing horns seems silly and ineffective. At best, such behavior might cause a bit of anxiety within the city, but it certainly does not seem like a plan for victory. Joshua was obedient nonetheless and followed God's instructions precisely.

> *Now the gates of Jericho were securely barred because of the Israelites. No one went out and no one came in. Then the LORD said to Joshua, "See, I have delivered Jericho into your hands, along with its king and its fighting men. March around the city once with all the armed men. Do this for six days. Have seven priests carry trumpets of rams' horns in front of the ark. On the seventh day, march around the city seven times, with the priests blowing the trumpets. When you hear them sound a long blast on the trumpets, have the whole army give a loud shout; then the wall of the city will collapse and the army will go up, everyone straight in."*
>
> — JOSHUA 6:1-5

As far as I know, there is no logical explanation for why city walls would fall because an army walked around them several times and yelled loudly. I have heard many theories, but none of them adequately explain how this occurred outside of supernatural intervention. We do know that the commander of the Lord's army was there with his sword drawn and ready for battle. Joshua encounters this angel in Joshua 5.

Now when Joshua was near Jericho, he looked up and saw a man standing in front of him with a drawn sword in his hand. Joshua went up to him and asked, "Are you for us or for our enemies?" "Neither," he replied, "but as commander of the army of the Lord I have now come." Then Joshua fell facedown to the ground in reverence, and asked him, "What message does my Lord have for his servant?" The commander of the LORD's army replied, "Take off your sandals, for the place where you are standing is holy." And Joshua did so.

— JOSHUA 5:13-15

After this encounter, God gave His instructions to Joshua. I can only imagine what was going on in the unseen spiritual realm. I believe God sent His warring angels to destroy the walls of Jericho so Israel could be victorious in battle. Could the circling of the city by the Israelites have been symbolic of angels surrounding the city in the spiritual realm? We do not know, but I believe the outcome of this battle would have been much different had Joshua ignored the strange directions of the Lord and attacked the city in a more conventional way. As intercessors, it is important to follow God's direction even when it seems strange or unusual.

Obedience Is Important

A biblical story that demonstrates the importance of performing prophetic gestures obediently comes from Numbers 20. As was common after the Israelites had escaped their slavery in Egypt, the people were complaining because they were facing a difficult situation. They were camped at the Desert of Zin, and there was not enough water for the people and their livestock. The people confronted Moses and Aaron, blaming them for leading them to this barren place with insufficient resources of water. Moses and Aaron retreated to the tent of meeting where Moses would talk with God and get guidance for leading the rebellious nation. While there, God told Moses to go out and gather the people together. Once they were assembled, Moses was to speak to a rock and water would pour forth, providing all that the people needed for their families and livestock to survive.

What is interesting is that Moses did as the Lord commanded him, except he struck the rock twice with his staff instead of speaking to it. Even so, the rock split open and water flowed from it because God was gracious and faithful to provide water despite the fact that He was upset with Moses' behavior. The text does not tell us why Moses chose to strike the rock instead of speaking to it, but his disobedience came with a consequence. I can imagine his frustration trying to lead such a challenging group of people, but if he acted out of anger or emotion, it did not please God. Consequently, Moses was not allowed to lead the Israelites into the Promised Land.

As this story demonstrates, obedience is crucial when prophetically gesturing during an intercession session. Moses did not precisely follow God's direction, and there were consequences. God always blesses obedience. We can only wonder what would have happened if Joshua became tired, bored, or impatient while walking around Jericho. Would God have still taken the city if Joshua only walked around five times on the final day? I cannot answer that, but it is clear that obedience is a key element when performing prophetic gestures and symbolism. Obedience demonstrates our love for God (John 14:15). As intercessors, we want to always follow His lead.

We should not disregard prophetic gestures out of fear of getting it wrong, but we should also not take them too far. If we do, the intercession session can lose focus and become self-indulgent. If we restrict prophetic gestures completely, we may miss out on some of the wonderful things God is directing us to do. These prophetic acts can be fun, but they should not become the main focus of what we do. Prophetic gestures are just another way we can partner with what God is doing as part of our intercessory prayer sessions.

When Riverlife outgrew our original church building, we

decided to purchase new property to build a larger facility. This process took many years, millions of dollars, and a multitude of prayers. When the time neared for us to break ground, most of the church met on the new property to thank God for what He had given us and to bless the property. Each attendee was given a small amount of oil to anoint the ground. People walked and prayed over nearly every foot of the property, pouring out oil as they went. This was a prophetic gesture symbolizing the presence and consecration of the Holy Spirit. As we prayed and poured out the oil, we invited the Holy Spirit to inhabit the boundaries of our property. I believe He accepted our invitation. No matter where you are on the church property, it is not difficult to become aware of His presence. From the farthest reaches of the parking lot to the pulpit on the stage, there is a tangible sense of the Holy Spirit's presence. God honored our obedience and regularly moves in supernatural ways through our congregation. I truly enjoyed that day because we did not limit this prophetic gesture to the intercessory prayer team. Everyone was invited to participate, and most of the church did.

You will have to determine what is acceptable and what is not for your church and faith tradition when it comes to prophetic gestures. They are not required to see God answer prayers, but they can be powerful when prompted by God. If God stirs your heart to act in a prophetic way as you pray, I encourage you to respond obediently. Follow His direction as precisely as you can. If God prompts you to walk around your church building a specific number of times, do it. Do not stop halfway through because you lose focus or become tired. Do not be afraid to act outside your comfort zone, either. Sometimes it feels weird—other times it seems like the natural thing to do. The key is to listen to God and obediently respond.

We cannot worry about embarrassing ourselves before God. King David did not worry about what others thought of him as he worshipped the Lord by dancing and singing wearing only an ephod (2 Sam. 6:14). Prophetic gestures may make us feel uncomfortable at times, but if God leads us to perform in a certain way, we should do so obediently. What seems like strange behavior to us may be accomplishing powerful things in the spiritual realm.

8

UTILIZING SPIRITUAL GIFTS WITHIN A TEAM

There are different kinds of gifts, but the same Spirit distributes them. There are different kinds of service, but the same Lord. There are different kinds of working, but in all of them and in everyone it is the same God at work. Now to each one the manifestation of the Spirit is given for the common good. To one there is given through the Spirit a message of wisdom, to another a message of knowledge by means of the same Spirit, to another faith by the same Spirit, to another gifts of healing by that one Spirit, to another miraculous powers, to another prophecy, to another distinguishing between spirits, to another speaking in different kinds of tongues, and to still another the interpretation of tongues. All these are the work of one and the same Spirit, and he distributes them to each one, just as he determines.

— 1 CORINTHIANS 12:4-11

GOD HAS CREATED A PHENOMENALLY DIVERSE HUMANITY. We are each unique and wonderful, and despite our diversity, we all come from a common origin—God the Father. I think He created each of us with unique characteristics, personalities, and giftings so we would interlock, making the church stronger as a sum of parts as opposed to functioning individually. We need each other to become greater than ourselves. Like pieces of a beautiful puzzle, when we come together, we complete God's picture of family.

God loves relationships and has set up the workings of humanity to require cooperation between us to live a full life and build His church. For ministry, God has given each of us different spiritual gifts. This distribution of gifts requires that the body of Christ operate in a complementary manner. Every believer has something of immense value to contribute. In God's family, no one is left out or unable to make a valuable contribution.

An intercessory prayer team is a microcosm of the greater church body, with each intercessor bringing a unique gift mix to the ministry of intercession. To become more effective as we intercede, it is essential to learn to use the diversity of gifts within the team. Each person and each gift contribute a key part to how effectively the team functions. If the team can figure out which gifts each team member operates in and how to utilize those gifts in cooperation with the other team members, the effectiveness of the team will increase substantially. This will also help build unity among the team as members complement and interact with one another.

In 1 Corinthians 12, we see that each of the gifts mentioned by Paul can be used in an intercessory prayer session. This is not an exhaustive list of spiritual gifts. Other passages mention additional gifts (Rom. 12:6-8, 1 Peter 4:10-11, Eph. 4:12), but the gifts mentioned in 1 Corinthians are commonly used within intercession, so I have focused on this passage specifically. Let's look at each of the gifts mentioned by Paul and how they can be utilized within a team.

The Gift of Wisdom

The main purpose of intercession is to understand what God's will is for a person or situation, agree with His will, and partner with God to see His will come to fruition. The spiritual nature of intercession requires that we think, act, and pray outside of our earthly paradigm, which is why the spiritual gift of wisdom is such a wonderful gift from God, especially for intercessors. The gift of wisdom comes from God through the Holy Spirit, Who empowers us to use this gift. *"This is what we speak, not in words taught us by human wisdom but in words taught by the Spirit, explaining spiritual realities with Spirit-taught words"* (1 Cor. 2:13). Earthly wisdom is good, but it is incredibly inferior to God's wisdom. *"For the foolishness of God is wiser than human wisdom, and the weakness of God is stronger than human strength"* (1 Cor. 1:25). God is a gracious god, and He will give us godly wisdom if we ask for it. *"If any of you lacks wisdom, you should ask God, who gives generously to all without finding fault, and it will be given to you"* (James 1:5).

The gift of wisdom is rooted in a deep knowledge and understanding of God's Word. *"Sanctify them by the truth; your word is truth"* (John 17:17). When we speak out of God's wisdom, it should impart understanding that guides us to the purposes of God and His truth. Truth in turn leads us to righteous living. A righteous life gives glory to God. Just as it leads us there, the application of the gift of wisdom should lead others to holiness and worship.

It is common for intercessors to pray for answers to problems. We want to know how God would solve a problem so we can partner with Him for the outcome, since He is the source of all wisdom and freely gives it to those who ask for it. God's answers are often not what we would come up with on our own. His wisdom cuts through the confusion and gives us the way forward. The gift of wisdom should always point us to the cross because the highest wisdom is found in the gospel of Jesus Christ. When we use the lens of the gospel to view life, we will clearly see the path we are to take.

It is at the foot of the cross that we find the answers to whatever we are facing.

The gift of wisdom helps us to see through the fog of our circumstances and points us to the truth of God's Word, which helps us to live in righteousness.

I have kept my feet from every evil path so that I might obey your word. I have not departed from your laws, for you yourself have taught me. How sweet are your words to my taste, sweeter than honey to my mouth! I gain understanding from your precepts; therefore I hate every wrong path. Your word is a lamp for my feet, a light on my path. I have taken an oath and confirmed it, that I will follow your righteous laws. I have suffered much; preserve my life, LORD according to your word.

— PSALM 119:101-107

An intercessor operating in the gift of wisdom can speak out the solution, which then allows the team to pray in agreement with the will of God.

The Gift of Knowledge

The spiritual gift of knowledge is similar to the gift of wisdom, which is why these two gifts often work closely together. Knowledge is a capacity to understand information and relate it to others in a way that points to truth. Like the gift of wisdom, the gift of knowledge is deeply grounded in God's Word. The application of this gift helps others gain understanding of God's Word and how to apply it in their lives. An intercessor operating in this gift would often contrast the situation that is being prayed for with relevant scripture passages as the Holy Spirit brings to mind the truth of God's Word.

The gift of knowledge also enables a person to "know" something that they previously did not know. The Holy Spirit supernaturally imparts knowledge to a believer about a person or circumstance that was not previously known by natural means. This sort of knowledge is not learned, but is given spiritually to an individual. An example of this comes from Mark 2.

A few days later, when Jesus again entered Capernaum, the people heard that he had come home. They gathered in such large numbers that there was no room left, not even outside the door, and he preached the word to them. Some men came, bringing to him a paralyzed man, carried by four of them. Since they could not get him to Jesus because of the crowd, they made an opening in the roof above Jesus by digging through it and then lowered the mat the man was lying on. When Jesus saw their faith, he said to the paralyzed man, "Son, your sins are forgiven." Now some teachers of the law were sitting there, thinking to themselves, "Why does this fellow talk like that? He's blaspheming! Who can forgive sins but God alone?" Immediately Jesus knew in his spirit that this was what they were thinking in their hearts, and he said to them, "Why are you thinking these things? Which is easier: to say to this paralyzed man, 'Your sins are forgiven,' or to say, 'Get up, take your mat and walk'? But I want you to know that the Son of Man has authority on earth to forgive sins." So he said to the man, "I tell you, get up, take your mat and go home." He got up, took his mat and walked out in full view of them all. This amazed everyone and they praised God, saying, "We have never seen anything like this!"

— MARK 2:1-12

This is the familiar story of Jesus healing a paralyzed man who was brought to Him by his friends. Initially, Jesus forgives the man of his sins because He sees the faith of the man's friends. This upsets the teachers of law because Jesus is declaring that He has the authority to forgive sins, which in their minds is blasphemy because only God has that authority. As they grumble silently to themselves, Jesus "knows" in His spirit what they are thinking in their hearts. This gift of knowledge allowed Jesus to confront the Jewish teachers and demonstrate His authority over sin and sickness by healing the paralyzed man. As a result, the crowd praised God.

In another example, Jesus speaks a word of knowledge over Nathanael.

The next day Jesus decided to leave for Galilee. Finding Philip, he said to him, "Follow me." Philip, like Andrew and Peter, was from the town of Bethsaida. Philip found Nathanael and told him, "We have found the one Moses wrote about in the Law, and about whom the prophets also wrote—Jesus of Nazareth, the son of Joseph."

"Nazareth! Can anything good come from there?" Nathanael asked. "Come and see," said Philip. When Jesus saw Nathanael approaching, he said of him, "Here truly is an Israelite in whom there is no deceit."

"How do you know me?" Nathanael asked. Jesus answered, "I saw you while you were still under the fig tree before Philip called you." Then Nathanael declared, "Rabbi, you are the Son of God; you are the king of Israel."

Jesus said, "You believe because I told you I saw you under the fig tree. You will see greater things than that." He then added, "Very truly I tell you, you will see 'heaven open, and the angels of God ascending and descending on' the Son of Man."

— JOHN 1:43-51

In this example, Jesus received two words of knowledge about Nathanael. First, He knew Nathanael was a man of integrity, calling him "an Israelite in whom there was no deceit." Secondly, He knew that Nathanael was sitting under a fig tree earlier in the day. Both words of knowledge came to Jesus through the Holy Spirit, as Jesus did not know Nathanael before this meeting and had not been around the fig tree. Jesus used these words of knowledge to call Nathanael as a disciple.

In intercession, the gift of knowledge may come as revelatory understanding that was not known beforehand. Like all spiritual gifts, the Holy Spirit is the One Who gives this knowledge to lead us to truth and ultimately to glorify God. When someone is given spiritual information (a word of knowledge) by God, that person has a responsibility to interpret and apply the information wisely. Often a word of knowledge is the key that unlocks a situation so that God's will is done. Someone with this gift must be in an intimate relationship with God and have a deep understanding of scripture.

Like the gift of wisdom, the gift of knowledge should inform others of God's truths and point them to righteousness.

For this reason, since the day we heard about you, we have not stopped praying for you. We continually ask God to fill you with the knowledge of his will through all the wisdom and understanding that the Spirit gives, so that you may live a life worthy of the Lord and please him in every way: bearing fruit in every good work, growing in the knowledge of God, being strengthened with all power according to his glorious might so that you may have great endurance and patience, and giving joyful thanks to the Father, who has qualified you to share in the inheritance of his holy people in the kingdom of light.

— COLOSSIANS 1:9-12

The Gift of Faith

Faith is a supernatural capacity to believe God. The gift of faith is a special gift for an intercessor because it is our faith in God that empowers our prayers. Praying in faith is powerful, as it allows us to believe that God is who He says He is, and He can do what He says He can do. *"Truly I tell you, if you have faith and do not doubt, not only can you do what was done to the fig tree, but also you can say to this mountain, 'Go, throw yourself into the sea,' and it will be done. If you believe, you will receive whatever you ask for in prayer"* (Matt. 21:21-22). The gift of faith is not to be confused with the faith to be saved (Eph. 2:8), although it is rooted in the faith of salvation that knows that we can trust Jesus and rely upon Him with our needs. The gift of faith is special because it usually precedes incredible works.

Those operating in the gift of faith pray with a firm belief that God is good and is working in the situation to bring about the best outcome, and with a deep certainty about who God is and what He has promised. They live with full confidence that their life is in God's hands, trusting that all things will work for their good (Rom. 8:28). This confidence enables them to pray boldly despite what they see or experience in the natural realm. Those with the gift of faith trust God more than they trust their own understanding and experience in the world, making their prayers powerful and effective. Intercessors with the gift of faith believe at the deepest level of their being that their prayers are heard, and that God is acting in response to their prayers. *"Therefore I tell you, whatever you ask for in prayer, believe that you have received it, and it will be yours"* (Mark 11:24). They also encourage others around them to believe. They can raise the "faith temperature" in the room because their whole life is centered around their relationship with God.

In Acts 3, Peter and John exercise the gift of faith as they heal a lame beggar. In this case, they did not pray for the man. They simply took his hand and commanded him to walk. If you can imagine the scene, grabbing a crippled man's hand and telling him to walk would take a supernatural kind of faith. Peter had been with Jesus and seen Him do miraculous works, and because of these past experiences, he had developed a gift of faith. At Peter's command, the man was healed and went through the temple jumping and running while praising God. The crowds were astonished at what happened and went to Peter and John in amazement. In response, Peter addressed the crowd. *"By faith in the name of Jesus, this man whom you see and know was made strong. It is Jesus' name and the faith that comes through him that has completely healed him, as you can all see"* (Acts 3:16).

The Gift of Healing

The spiritual gift of healing is a powerful and mysterious gift. A person with this gift has great compassion and faith to pray for the sick and injured, knowing that supernatural healing is one of the benefits of being a child of God. Therefore, they can pray with a deep belief that the sick person will be healed and are not discouraged when healing does not happen because they understand that the power and choice to heal rest on God's sovereign shoulders. Those operating in the gift of healing see divine healing occur more regularly than someone who occasionally prays for healing. Like the gifts of wisdom and knowledge, the gift of healing often pairs with the gift of faith. Obviously, it requires a great amount of faith to pray for healing, but those with this gift trust God deeply and exercise this gift in obedience, leaving the outcome in God's hands.

Intercessors are often called upon to pray for someone's physical needs. Yet, the gift of healing often results in spiritual healing as well as physical healing. God will use physical healing to demonstrate His love toward a person so they might be saved. Spiritual healing is far more important than physical healing. Physical healing is temporary, as we will all die eventually at some point. Spiritual healing, or salvation, impacts a person for eternity. Perhaps the greatest miracle is when a sinner is reconciled to God through Jesus Christ. Those with the gift of healing can be used by God to meet those needs and point the person to the source of all healing —God.

As Jesus went on from there, two blind men followed him, calling out, "Have mercy on us, Son of David!" When he had gone indoors, the blind men came to him, and he asked them, "Do you believe that I am able to do this?" "Yes,

Lord," they replied. Then he touched their eyes and said, "According to your faith let it be done to you"; and their sight was restored. Jesus went through all the towns and villages, teaching in their synagogues, proclaiming the good news of the kingdom and healing every disease and sickness.

— MATTHEW 9:27-30, 35

The Gift of Miracles

The spiritual gift of miracles is another mysterious gift. The term "miracles" can be quite broad and at times, subjective. However, Jesus said,

And these signs will accompany those who believe: In my name they will drive out demons; they will speak in new tongues; they will pick up snakes with their hands; and when they drink deadly poison, it will not hurt them at all; they will place their hands on sick people, and they will get well."

— MARK 16:17-18

As you can see from this passage, miracles might include healing, tongues, deliverance, supernatural health, and even resurrection from the dead. The miraculous is mysterious because it defies our reason. For instance, water does not become wine on its own (John 2:1-12). In any case, miracles should accompany those who believe. Christians should expect to see miracles occur in the name of Jesus. In 2 Kings 4, we see a miracle occur to help a widow pay off her debts after her husband dies. The prophet Elisha instructs the widow to collect as many jars as she can from neighbors and friends. Although she only has a small jar of olive oil at her disposal, Elisha tells her to pour the olive oil from her jar into the empty jars. This creates a miracle, as the small jar of olive oil fills multiple jars.

The wife of a man from the company of the prophets cried out to Elisha, "Your servant my husband is dead, and you know that he revered the LORD. But now his creditor is coming to take my two boys as his slaves." Elisha replied to her, "How can I help you? Tell me, what do you have in your house?" "Your servant has nothing there at all," she said, "except a small jar of olive oil." Elisha said, "Go around and ask all your neighbors for empty jars. Don't ask for just a few. Then go inside and shut the door behind you and your sons. Pour oil into all the jars, and as each is filled, put it to one side." She left him and shut the door behind her and her sons. They brought the jars to her and she kept pouring. When all the jars were full, she said to her son, "Bring me another one." But he replied, "There is not a jar left." Then the oil stopped flowing. She went and told the man of God, and he said, "Go, sell the oil and pay your debts. You and your sons can live on what is left."

— 2 KINGS 4:1-7

Like other spiritual gifts, the gift of miracles is empowered by the Holy Spirit and requires great faith. I believe the gift of miracles is given by God to accomplish His will and point humanity to His love. Unlike other spiritual gifts, the gift of miracles seems to be given at certain times and is not always immediately available to the believer. Often, miracles follow times of diligent prayer petitioning God to release His power into a situation. As intercessors, we should all press in for the miraculous, always trusting God and relying fully on Him for a miracle to occur.

The Gift of Prophecy

Paul encourages all believers to desire the gift of prophecy, as it is a wonderful gift from God for His children. *"Follow the way of love and eagerly desire gifts of the Spirit, especially prophecy"* (1 Cor. 14:1). The gift of prophecy is an encouraging gift to the church given to strengthen, encourage, and comfort those who receive it (1 Cor. 14). It is a gift that enables a person to hear God's words and see His hand at work so they may agree and declare it to the church. God releases revelatory information through prophecy to build up His church and see it flourish.

It is important to understand that prophecy is not limited only to select believers recognized as prophets. All believers can receive prophetic revelation through the Holy Spirit, and every Christian has the capacity to prophesy. We can all hear His voice because we are His sheep, and He is our shepherd. *"My sheep listen to my voice; I know them, and they follow me"* (John 10:27). This can cause trepidation for some believers. How can we know when a prophetic word is authentically from the Lord? The key is to test all prophecies. *"Do not treat prophecies with contempt but test them all; hold on to what is good, reject every kind of evil"* (1 Thess. 5:20-22). We must test the prophecies we receive as well as those spoken over the church. Paul encourages us to hold on to what is good and let go of what is not. This requires us to be wise and mature as we weigh a prophetic word.

Prophetic words are powerful and influential. They express the heart of God and are meant to build up the church. At times, they can be directive or corrective if required, but most often they are encouraging and provide an invitation from God to partner with Him in His purposes.

1 Corinthians 13:9 reminds us that *"...we know in part and prophesy in part."* This means that prophetic words can be limited and do not share God's entire plan. However, they do give us a glimpse into God's heart and what He wants to accomplish. The gift of prophecy used through intercession allows us to pray in agreement with God's plans and the direction that He is leading.

Prophecy must always be wrapped in love and humility. In fact, love should be our greatest motivation when prophesying. A prophetic word should push an individual or group forward toward the fullness of God's purposes for them. Paul reminds Timothy of the prophecies that had been spoken over him in the past to strengthen him in the work he was currently doing. *"Timothy, my son, I am giving you this command in keeping with the prophecies once made about you, so that by recalling them you may fight the battle well"* (1 Tim. 1:18). Prophetic words can bring us encouragement in the challenging times between when they are given and when they are fulfilled so we can stay focused on God's plans.

The Gift of Discernment

The gift of discernment is an incredible gift for an intercessor. Sometimes this gift can be called "discerning of spirits" because it allows a believer to determine which spirit is operating in a situation. The value of the gift of discernment is that there is a supernatural ability to determine evil from good or darkness from light. An intercessor operating in this gift can determine by the Holy Spirit whether the source of a situation is from God, Satan, the world, or another source. At times, this gift can operate as a seeing gift. The person can spiritually see the angelic and the demonic, which proves to be incredibly helpful when interceding. 1 John reminds us, *"Dear friends, do not believe every spirit, but test the spirits to see whether they are from God, because many false prophets have gone out into the world"* (1 John 4:1).

An example of someone operating in this gift is Paul in the book of Acts. Although the spirit was saying the right things, it was not a godly spirit. Paul discerned this and rebuked the spirit.

Once when we were going to the place of prayer, we were met by a female slave who had a spirit by which she predicted the future. She earned a great deal of money for her owners by fortune-telling. She followed Paul and the rest of us, shouting, "These men are servants of the Most High God, who are telling you the way to be saved." She kept this up for many days. Finally, Paul became so annoyed that he turned around and said to the spirit, "In the name of Jesus Christ I command you to come out of her!" At that moment the spirit left her.

— ACTS 16:16-18

When an intercessor operates in this gift, he or she can quickly determine how to pray because they are able to discern what is from the enemy and what is from God. This can help the team use the displacement principle and focus on what God is saying and doing instead of dealing with darkness directly. If they are a seer, an intercessor can also build the faith of the group by sharing what they are seeing in the spiritual realm. Often, those with a seer gift can give a commentary much like a sports announcer, detailing what is happening in the spiritual realm so the team can intercede accordingly.

The Gift of Tongues

The spiritual gift of tongues is unique among the other gifts, as it glorifies God through a spiritual language that is not known by the speaker. The Greek word for tongues is "glossolalia." This type of tongue is often referred to as a spiritual prayer language that a believer can utilize in their personal prayer life. Unlike other gifts, the gift of tongues tends to benefit the individual rather than the body of the church. It is a prayer language that is primarily focused on communicating with God personally. *"For anyone who speaks in a tongue does not speak to people but to God. Indeed, no one understands them; they utter mysteries by the Spirit"* (1 Cor. 14:2). Paul also goes on to say, *"Anyone who speaks in a tongue edifies themselves, but the one who prophesies edifies the church"* (1 Cor. 14:4).

In this way, tongues can be a gift that strengthens a believer personally, but does not edify the church as other gifts such as prophecy do. This does not mean that the gift of tongues should be less desired than the other gifts.

When the gift of tongues is spoken out into the body of Christ, interpretation of that tongue can edify the church. Interpretation is required because glossolalia is an unknown spiritual language, and those who hear it will not understand what is being said without interpretation. The gift of interpreting tongues can be a separate gift to the gift of tongues, or not. One person may speak, and another interpret, or the one speaking in tongues can also interpret what God was saying through them. Paul emphasizes the importance of interpretation in 1 Corinthians 14.

Now, brothers and sisters, if I come to you and speak in tongues, what good will I be to you, unless I bring you some revelation or knowledge or prophecy or word of instruction? Even in the case of lifeless things that make sounds, such as the pipe or harp, how will anyone know what tune is being played unless there is a distinction in the notes? Again, if the trumpet does not sound a clear call, who will get ready for battle? So, it is with you. Unless you speak intelligible words with your tongue, how will anyone know what you are saying? You will just be speaking into the air. Undoubtedly there are all sorts of languages in the world, yet none of them is without meaning. If then I do not grasp the meaning of what someone is saying, I am a foreigner to the speaker, and the speaker is a foreigner to me. So, it is with you. Since you are eager for gifts of the Spirit, try to excel in those that build up the church. For this reason, the one who speaks in a tongue should pray that they may interpret what they say. For if I pray in a tongue, my spirit prays, but my mind is unfruitful. So, what shall I do? I will pray with my spirit, but I will also pray with my understanding; I will sing with my spirit, but I will also sing with my understanding. Otherwise, when you are praising God in the Spirit, how can someone else, who is now put in the position of an inquirer, say "Amen" to your thanksgiving, since they do not know what you are saying? You are giving thanks well enough, but no one else is edified. I thank God that I speak in tongues more than all of you. But in the church I would rather speak five intelligible words to instruct others than ten thousand words in a tongue.

— 1 CORINTHIANS 14:6-19

As can be understood by Paul's explanation above, we must operate in the gift of tongues in an orderly and informed manner. I believe that some denominations have erroneously placed too much emphasis on this gift as evidence of being baptized in the Holy Spirit. To operate in any of the gifts requires the Holy Spirit's empowerment. Tongues, I believe, may not be given to every believer, but that does not mean that those who do not speak in tongues are not empowered by the Holy Spirit or baptized in His presence.

If you are not aware of which gifts you carry, I would strongly encourage you to find a spiritual gifts evaluation, take it, and examine the results. There are many such evaluations available online and at your local Christian bookstore. These evaluations are not always completely accurate, but can give a clear indication that you might be operating in certain giftings. It is well worth your time to discover and cultivate your spiritual gifts, especially if you are called to intercession. Each of us has a unique part to contribute to the body of Christ. This is how the church is meant to function. If we are not using our spiritual gifts, the church suffers for it.

Spiritual gifts are given by God for the edification of the church. Within an intercessory prayer team, the use of spiritual gifts is essential. Learning to cooperate with other intercessors that have different giftings will make a team much more effective and powerful. Cooperation helps to cultivate unity, which is vitally important for the ministry of intercession. Therefore, discover your gift or gifts and intentionally work to develop them as an intercessor. Then work together with other intercessors to see God's will done on the earth and to build His church.

9

PRACTICAL MATTERS

When God's supernatural power invades our earthly experience during intercession, it is both exciting and exhilarating. To experience moments like these requires that you take the organizational steps necessary to establish how your team will function by laying a foundational groundwork. Establishing the ways your team will function gives everyone a sense of safety and satisfaction as they serve. When you come together to intercede, you want to make the most of the time you have. Your team members have sacrificed their time to attend, and you do not want to waste this offering by being unprepared or disorganized. I believe this chapter will help new team leaders establish the culture and protocols they need, as well as providing some new insights and resources to help existing team leaders function more efficiently and productively. Developing ground rules, prayers to open and close a session, clear communication, and shared cultural values will enable your team to work with a focused unity. These protocols and practical matters will also build in a rhythm for your team's week-to-week functioning. People like to know what to expect when they serve.

Developing Core Values

You should begin this process by asking yourself a few questions. The first question should be, "What are the cultural values I want the team to reflect?" Since team unity is vital to the effectiveness of any team, when you and the team value the same things, it makes team unity much easier to cultivate. As you begin an intercessory prayer session, here are some other questions to consider:

What are the things you want the team to value as they interact with you, the church, the topic, and with each other?

Does everyone pray over each other in a cacophony of prayer? Or does one person pray at a time?

Is your team motivated by love, or are they there for other reasons?

Can anyone join the team, or is there a process they need to go through to determine their commitment and character ahead of time?

When conflicts arise, who ultimately handles their resolution?

These and many other questions need to be answered to develop a cultural values list and establish how your team will operate each time you meet. Once you know the culture you want to set, it becomes easy to weigh every intercessory prayer session's impact against what you are about.

My church's worship team has a cultural values list that our worship pastor often refers to during team meetings. He has developed a few simple statements that help each member of the team stay focused on what is important as they lead worship each week. It does not matter whether they are playing an instrument, streaming the service to the internet, or running the words on the screen—we are all working toward the same goal with an attitude in line with the established cultural values. It becomes obvious when someone is not in alignment with the core values of the team, as they usually become a distraction from what we are about.

The worship team's core values dictate what we focus on and what we minimize. For instance, we prioritize the presence of Jesus above all else because we meet each Sunday to worship Him. This means that we put our worship and ministry to Jesus above our plans, preparation, set list, or any other element when we gather for corporate worship. If some element of our service would draw attention away from our focus on Jesus, we choose to sacrifice that element without regret. Our primary purpose is to give God the glory, praise, and adoration He deserves.

Another core value of the team is that we seek to be authentically excellent. This means that we do not sweat a wrong note or mistake, but we also want to bring our best effort as we lead the congregation in worship. Although we value preparation and practice, perfection is not our measure of success. We all realize that we are not the focus of the service. We are there to give God glory and praise. We do our best in the role we are filling, but there is grace when things do not go as planned. No one is scolded for making a mistake. We all make every effort to do our part well so as not to be a distraction from the worship.

These are our worship team's cultural values:

- We prioritize the presence of Jesus with us above all else.
- We celebrate making room for Him and taking risks.
- We seek to be authentically excellent.
- We celebrate and strive for family.
- We recognize we are not our gift and value growth and feedback.

- We recognize that our platform is for service and not for spotlight.
- We want our lives to represent Jesus off the stage just as much as on it.
- We desire that what we cultivate would extend beyond our walls.

These core values determine how our worship team functions, what is important, and how it should look every Sunday. If a musician arrives on Sunday morning for sound check completely unprepared for the songs the worship leader has chosen, they have not met all of the values the team has agreed are important. Their lack of preparation may cause the rest of the team to have to operate outside of some of the values as well. The team may not be able to make room for a spontaneous Holy Spirit moment because the unprepared musician cannot play his or her part, which becomes a distraction. This may cause stress for the rest of the team and take the focus off the primary purpose of worshipping God. Suddenly the focus becomes about helping the unprepared person. In this kind of a scenario, things can quickly spiral. Although an intercessory prayer team may not operate on a stage in front of everyone like a worship team does, adhering to established core values is just as important for intercession to be effective.

I strongly encourage you to develop your own list of cultural values for your team. If you have an established team, introducing a list of values can help galvanize what you are trying to achieve. It will highlight the team members who should be involved and those who should not. Do not be afraid to hit the reset button if you need to. It is better to have conflict once than to have continuous conflict every time you meet. If someone is not willing to commit and conform to the cultural values of your team, it is better if they are not involved because they will only create disunity and distractions, neither of which are beneficial. As you develop your list of cultural values, take time to pray and wait on the Lord. He will show you what should be included. Also, think about the cultural values that your church holds as an organization. You want the intercessors to align with those greater values of your church as well as the values of the team.

Here are the cultural values I established for the intercessory prayer team that I led:

1. Team Unity – we recognize that each team member is uniquely gifted and valuable to the team. We demonstrate honor and compassion to each team member and the team leader. We strive to resolve disagreements or offense quickly by following the model of conflict resolution set out in Matthew 18. We want to serve the church motivated by love for one another, so we place our

opinions and preferences behind our purpose to intercede.

2. Personal Humility – we recognize that our role as intercessors is a serving role. We want to demonstrate honor, respect, and love to those we serve and serve alongside. We value others greater than ourselves (Phil. 2:3). We also submit to the authorities who have been placed over us. We honor leadership by faithfully following their lead.

3. Spiritual Maturity – those serving as intercessors should be mature disciples able to function in their spiritual gifts, submitted to authority, and knowledgeable in the Word. We recognize that we must prioritize personal intimacy with God to hear His voice clearly, agree with His purposes, and declare His will through intercession.

4. Spiritual Integrity – we recognize that spiritual warfare is a primary activity of intercession. We must keep short personal accounts with God. We do not want sin to become habitual and give the enemy a foothold in our life. We also recognize we have been given boundaries of authority to operate in. We recognize that it is wise to remain within those boundaries unless clearly directed by God.

5. Confidentiality – we recognize that many issues

we are asked to pray for are confidential in nature. We will not share these issues with others as gossip or in an inappropriate manner that may cause hurt or offense. We realize that our role as intercessors carries great responsibility. We honor that responsibility by keeping confidential matters within the team.

For me, these five core values are vital to the intercessory prayer team functioning in a manner that honors the leadership and serves the congregation. They are simple values, but each one speaks to what is required for an intercessor to serve effectively and with integrity. Your list may look completely different than mine, which is totally fine. Every church and every team will have its own flavor and emphasis. I have shared my list as an example to help you develop your own list. What is important is that team values reflect and support the cultural values of the church you are serving and are in alignment with the Bible.

New Team Members

Another practical matter is to determine who will serve as intercessors. Do you allow everyone who expresses interest in joining the team to be involved? Is there an application process they must go through? Do you recruit certain individuals to join the team? I have used all three of these options at separate times. In the past, I had an open-door policy for joining the team, which produced mixed results. Some weeks, a new person would turn up and it became a distraction as they did not have a commitment to the team, which meant they were not accountable to anyone and unaware of the cultural values that the consistent members operated in. Other times, a new attendee would simply sit in the corner without contributing to the session in a meaningful way, feeling out of place or too insecure to participate. I also became aware of the danger of sharing confidential information with someone who may or may not return the next week and who lacked accountability, so I decided I needed to build the team in a different way.

Here are some of my recommendations for building a team. First, use an application process to determine who is eligible to join the team. Although willing volunteers are sometimes hard to come by, using a well-thought-out application can prevent future conflicts and help develop a committed and capable team. An application gives you an opportunity to state the cultural values and expectations before a commitment is made by the prospective team member. It lets people know what they are signing up for in advance. As the team leader, an application also gives you a degree of insight into the person's intentions and ability before they become a member of your team. All of this requires forethought in the development of the application.

When developing an application, it is important to ask

the right questions. Begin by collecting the normal information, such as contact details and any prior experience. Ask questions that reveal a person's heart, suitability, and commitment to the team. Include a section where they share their testimony of becoming a Christian. Ask if they are serving in other areas of your church. If someone is over-committed, they may not attend consistently, which can impact your team especially if you have a small team. Ask if they are church members and how long they have been a part of your church. I looked for intercessors who had been a part of the church for at least six months before joining the team so I could see if they had settled into our church and wanted to stay long term. Church membership need not necessarily be a requirement, but it does demonstrate that a person has committed to your church. Finally, I like to include a statement that highlights how being an intercessor is a privilege that carries great responsibility. That privilege may not be perpetual if a team member does not uphold the rules and cultural values of the team. By stating this up front, you have an out if certain team members are causing disunity and disruption. Raising expectations and responsibilities can result in a committed and impactful group of intercessors. Those who are not prepared to meet your expectations are weeded out early in the process, which greatly aids in developing team unity.

Ground Rules

Ground rules are the protocols and practical behaviors your team members are expected to follow when participating as intercessors to help your sessions run smoothly in an organized manner. These rules do not need to be posted in the room where you pray, but they should be discussed at the beginning of each year or at your first meeting. Each team member should understand and agree to follow these rules, as they enable the team to function effectively. Asking each team member to sign a group commitment puts their agreement in writing, demonstrating their understanding of how they are expected to participate on the team. I would suggest that this list be brief but inclusive of everything that you need to lead your team effectively. These rules often reflect your cultural values. You may want to address issues such as confidentiality, punctuality, submission to authority, and mutual respect.

Confidentiality

For me, confidentiality is vital within an intercessory prayer team. When I was leading a team, I was often given topics to intercede for that were delicate and sensitive in nature. Maybe a pastor was struggling personally and wanted to be prayed for, but did not want his or her struggles to be broadcast to the wider church. The intercessors must be able to keep this type of information to themselves outside of the intercession session. If each team member is not committed to confidentiality, a lot of damage can be done through careless words. This also highlights the need for each team member to be a mature Christian. If anyone has a lingering offense toward a pastor, they may use the confidential information they learned at the intercession session against that pastor with potentially devastating results. Confidentiality must be observed. Otherwise, the team will lose all credibility.

Punctuality

Another ground rule I included for my team was punctuality. If the intercession session begins at 7:30 p.m. team members should try to arrive prior to that time. This might be a personal pet peeve of mine, but waiting on late team members means you must either postpone starting your intercessory prayer session or repeat any essential information when they finally arrive. Both actions waste other team members' time and abbreviates the time you have to intercede. Punctuality may not seem like a significant issue, but the impact of team members trickling in at various times does distract from the focus of the intercessory prayer session.

Submission to Authority

Submission to authority and authority structures have been addressed at length earlier in this book. I will not belabor the topic here. However, I will remind you that a mature understanding of authority and where each person fits within the hierarchy aids in the way an intercessory prayer session functions. If each team member knows their position in the hierarchy of authority within the spiritual and earthly realms, their prayers will avoid overstepping the established boundaries, thereby preventing blowback from the enemy when ground is taken for the kingdom. On a practical level, recognizing who the team leader is and following their lead establishes order within the team. There cannot be multiple captains and no sailors. There must be someone making decisions and directing the team. You will not make much progress if there is confusion about who the leader is. When each team member is submitted to authority, the team will run smoothly and conflicts will be minimized.

Mutual Respect

In 2009, Danny Silk published a book called *Culture of Honor* in which he encourages Christians to demonstrate honor for one another. He states, "A culture of honor is created when a community learns how to discern and receive people in their God-given identity" (p. 39). This means that we try to see each other the way God sees us and created us. When we demonstrate mutual respect for one another based on our God-given identity, each person will feel valued and capable of contributing in a meaningful way. This ground rule verges on being a cultural value, but when demonstrated consistently, it makes the running of the team much easier. Diversity is inevitable within a church congregation. We are all unique and uniquely gifted. Honoring that diversity brings unity and strengthens the team because everyone has something of significance to contribute.

These are only a few examples of ground rules that you might want to include for your team to function week to week. Often, ground rules are more about attitudes and perspectives than proper do-this-don't-do-that kind of rules. If each team member is committed to the role of intercessor and willing to honor the cultural values and ground rules of the team, the team will function effectively and smoothly, unify quickly, and stay focused on their responsibility. In this kind of an environment, leaders can lead more effectively. While ground rules do not eliminate every conflict or issue, they do establish the normal operation for the team while providing a sense of stability and predictability for the team as they give their time to serve.

Opening Prayer of Protection

Spiritual warfare is a necessary activity as an intercessor. We believe that prayer is powerful, and as such, we use prayer as a weapon against the enemy, to tear down his strongholds and see God's will done. We cannot intercede effectively if we are not confronting the enemy through spiritual warfare.

Since we are often frontline soldiers, we must be wise and diligent to protect ourselves from the attacks of the enemy. Therefore, I recommend opening and closing every intercession session with a strategic prayer to protect the team. I instituted this practice when I saw the enemy take advantage of some of the more vulnerable members periodically. Team members should not suffer from demonic attack because leadership did not take the necessary precautions.

When you open with a prayer of protection, do not do it out of fear or habit, but with intentionality, recognizing that we are confronting powerful spiritual strongholds when we intercede. Just as a soldier would not go into battle without first equipping himself, we do not want to engage in spiritual warfare unprepared (Eph. 6:10-17). A prayer of protection does not need to be long or complicated, but it does need to cover certain aspects that will spiritually cover your team as you intercede. It is best to have the team leader lead the prayer, as he or she is the spiritual authority within the team. Some aspects I recommend including in an opening prayer are to spiritually seal the room, remove any darkness inhabiting the space, and ask the Holy Spirit to fill the room with His presence and light. Additionally, I would forbid the enemy from watching, listening, or interfering with the intercessory prayer session in any way. Here is a sample of an opening prayer:

In Jesus' name, we command every spirit and power of darkness to leave this room. In Jesus' name, we ask that the room be sealed spiritually so that the enemy cannot see, hear, or interfere with the work we are doing. Holy Spirit, we invite You to fill this room, and each one of us, with Your light, love, and presence. We ask that You cover us from any attack of the enemy as we intercede. Cover us under Your wing, Lord. Purify our hearts as we pray. Tune our eyes and ears to Your hand and voice that we may clearly see and hear what You are doing and saying. We give You praise and thanks in advance for what You are going to accomplish through this session. In Jesus' name, amen.

As you can see, this is not a lengthy prayer, but it does address specific areas that need to be covered. Issues such as spiritual protection, purity, and focus are key elements that are needed in every intercessory prayer session. There may be other areas that you want to include as you develop your own opening prayer. While using an opening prayer does not guarantee that there will be no challenge from the enemy, it does set up a spiritual environment that is easier to function in. I recommend that you encourage each intercessor to check their heart before interceding to see if there is any unconfessed sin or offense. Coming with a pure heart eliminates opportunities for the enemy to distract or disrupt your intercessory prayer sessions.

Closing Prayer of Protection

Like the opening prayer, a closing prayer should also be intentional and focus on certain issues that will protect your team. It does not need to be a lengthy prayer, but may need to be adapted each week depending on the topics that were prayed for. For instance, a closing prayer may be different after spending most of your intercessory prayer session praying for divine healing for someone. This type of intercession may not entail a lot of spiritual warfare. In contrast, if you spent most of the evening conducting spiritual warfare directly, you might want to close the session with extra prayers of protection for the team. Again, this does not mean you are responding out of fear. However, we know the enemy will take advantage of any opportunity to attack a Christian, especially after he [the enemy] has lost ground that he previously held. Wise caution and fear are two quite different things. Make sure that your closing prayer is appropriate for the type of intercessory prayer session that was conducted. Here is a sample closing prayer that I would use after conducting a significant amount of spiritual warfare:

> Thank You, Jesus, for the victory that You won on the cross and by Your resurrection. We ask that You now release us from this time of intercession. Please cleanse each team member in the blood of Jesus. Please remove every authority of darkness that would like to attach to us. In Jesus' name, we forbid any retaliation against us, our families, our possessions, or the things we care about. Surround us in Your love and displace any hidden fear in our thoughts. Please refresh and refill each one as they have served. In Jesus' name, amen.

The intent of this prayer is to put the enemy on notice that we will not accept any retaliation for what was prayed for. We are not going to partner with the enemy's fear or lies. Bear in mind that each intercessory prayer session should remain within the boundaries of spiritual authority (see previous chapters on understanding authority). If those boundaries are observed properly, the enemy should not have much, if any, authority to push back against the members of your team.

A closing prayer of protection becomes the final statement of defeat toward the enemy when the team has used their delegated authority appropriately. It is impossible to know what is in everyone's hearts, but if your team has been trained well and understands the hierarchy of spiritual authority, there should be minimal spiritual attack from the enemy.

Instituting an opening and closing prayer of protection is highly encouraged because of the nature of intercession. There is often spiritual warfare required to shift the works of the enemy so that God's will may be done. The opening prayer sets the tone for the intercession session, and the closing prayer sets the tone for the rest of the week. One prepares our hearts and minds to wage spiritual battle, and the other cleanses us from the remnants of the fight. Each prayer is intentional and valuable. If you have not previously used an opening and closing prayer of protection for your sessions, now is the time. I believe you will see a difference in the effectiveness of your team and a reduction of individual spiritual warfare that each team member must endure.

Who shall separate us from the love of Christ? Shall trouble or hardship or persecution or famine or nakedness or danger or sword? As it is written: "For your sake we face *death all day long; we are considered as sheep to be slaughtered."* No, in all these things we are more than conquerors through him who loved us. For I am convinced that neither death nor life, neither angels nor demons, neither the present nor the future, nor any powers, neither height nor depth, nor anything else in all creation, will be able to separate us from the love of God that is in Christ Jesus our Lord.*

— ROMANS 8:35-39

Communication

As a leader, you are always communicating with your team. Whether it is the details of the next meeting, sharing the topics that the team will intercede for, or resolving conflicts, communication is the tool that must be used to lead the team. Sharing information does not necessarily equate to effective communication. Your team wants to understand the full meaning of the information that you share. They want to know how the information impacts them and how they should respond to the information appropriately. Effective communication leaves your team feeling confident in their role, informed about their responsibilities, and secure in their position on the team. Strong communicators can cast a vision in a way that makes others want to follow with enthusiasm and loyalty. Communication is one of the building blocks on which a team is built. Without effective communication, like the proverbial house built on the sand, it does not take much pressure to crumble and fall.

It is important to find the most effective ways to communicate with your team. This may take some experimentation. In the past, email revolutionized how we communicated with one another. Today, the sheer volume of emails we must wade through each day makes email less effective as a form of communication. In my experience, very few of my team members read my emails, and those who did failed to retain the information very well. This is not to say that email is useless, but now there are other forms of communication that seem to be more effective. If you do use email as your primary form of communication, it is important that you keep it brief and to the point. You want to put the most important information at the top of the email. That way, if a team member only reads the first paragraph, they have seen the most important points you want to get across. I would not send an email with more than two to three paragraphs at a time. The sad fact is that most people will not read it to the end. Email is an easy means of communicating with your team, but you may need to be more creative with your communication if you are not seeing the results you want.

Developing a team-specific chat group on one of the numerous messaging apps has proven effective for me in recent years. Using a group messaging app can be advantageous over email because it is topic specific. When a team member receives a message on the group app, they know it is about the intercessory prayer team. The danger of these apps is that everyone on team can reply. Some people are chattier than others and will inundate the message board with comments that may not be focused on the purpose of the group. When this happens, the initial message can be lost as other team members must scroll up to find the main message that spawned the multitude of replies. To prevent this, some ground rules can be applied. You can ask your team not to reply to those messages unless you specifically request it. Be sure to communicate the reasons that the chat group is not to be used for idle chat so you do not offend anyone. You can have one message group set up to be your communication vehicle and another group for those on your team who want to chat or share. Interaction between team members is a wonderful thing, but when it prohibits clear communication from being distributed, it must be minimized or diverted to an alternative place.

Person-to-person communication is still the best way to communicate with your team. The inhibiting factor of this form of communication is time. Most of us are time-poor so we have all gravitated to electronic forms of communication. Electronic communication is convenient, but as I have discussed, it may not always be effective. The best time to communicate with your team is when you are with them personally. Face-to-face communication is powerful, whether it be one-on-one or to a group. People are still wired to read body language, listen to the tone and timbre of your voice, and watch your facial expressions. None of these things are possible through electronic forms of communication. In-person communication expresses so much more than typed words on a page.

Remember, sharing information is not the same as communicating. We must take advantage of the opportunities we get when we meet to communicate our most vital information. Setting a time during each intercession session for updates and important information can go a long way in making your team feel informed and in the loop. Your team can ask questions and clarify anything they do not understand. I would also encourage you to make the time to call each of your team members regularly. It does not have to be each week, but calling them once a term makes them feel important and valued. Personal communication is always best. It is worth every minute it consumes.

Communicating with Leadership

Open communication lines need to be established between you and the senior pastor, other pastoral staff, and the church's governing body, such as the eldership or deacons where applicable. These leaders need to know that they can come to the intercessory prayer team with their needs and that they will be prayed for. This requires good relationships between the team leader and those in leadership. At the best of times, leaders can be guarded about their personal and ministry needs. Confidentiality must be a priority when you receive a prayer request. Some leaders may feel vulnerable when sharing a prayer request. The intercessory prayer team must handle every request with honor and maturity. The reputation of the team is established by how well it handles sensitive requests with confidentiality and care.

In addition to receiving prayer requests, it is important to communicate the outcome of the intercession session to the leadership. Was there a word of knowledge or wisdom given to help navigate a difficult situation? Is there a testimony to share? The leadership will want to know what the intercessors discovered as they prayed. As the team leader, you will need to know the best ways of passing information back to the leadership. Do they prefer email? Do they prefer a phone call? Do they want you to write out a summary of the session? These are great questions to ask. It is to everyone's benefit to establish a clear and open means of communicating back and forth. If it is done well, the intercessors will be seen as an incredible blessing and asset of the church. If done badly, they can become a thorn in the flesh.

Conflicts and Communication

As a pastor or team leader, you will face conflicts between yourself and those on the team as well as between team members. If you remain in leadership for any duration, you will have to deal with conflict at some point. Conflict cannot be avoided, but you can control how it is dealt with and resolved. It is particularly important to know the chain of authority when resolving conflicts. Who has the authority to make decisions, enforce discipline, and establish the outcomes? If you are a volunteer team leader, you will most likely have less authority to do these things than if you are a pastor on the church staff. This does not mean that a volunteer team leader is powerless, but it does mean that a volunteer will need to lean on a pastor more when conflicts arise. Consequently, developing strong and respectful relationships with those in leadership over you is essential.

I have been involved in ministry leadership in many different roles for over thirty years. I have served both as a volunteer and as a paid member of the church staff. Over the years, I have learned that every leader needs to know that those in authority over them have their back and will support them when conflicts arise. I believe this is one of the most important dynamics that needs to be established. This does not mean that the person above you must always take your side or agree with you, but you need to know that they will work alongside you to bring resolution to the conflict in a way that considers both sides fairly. You do not want to be thrown under the bus or made to be the sacrificial lamb to end a conflict quickly. If you are a pastor, does the senior pastor have your back? If you are a volunteer leader, does your supervising pastor support you? If not, you could be in a precarious position. If so, you are truly blessed.

Once again, communication is the greatest tool that a leader can use to avoid conflicts and direct their team effectively. Conflicts often result from a lack of communication or miscommunication. When things are left unsaid or come across in a confusing manner, it leaves the door open for conflicts to emerge. All leaders must be competent communicators. Those following your leadership need to be regularly informed of what is happening and where you are going as a team. Those above you in leadership will want to stay informed of how the team is doing and if there are issues that need to be addressed. Effective communication creates an environment of transparency. Transparency creates trust. Trust is required to keep relationships healthy and moving forward. Developing the paths of communication with your team and with your superiors is essential to avoid conflict. Bad communication is one the most significant enemies to your team's success and unity.

Developing the protocols and procedures that you need to support the practical matters of team leadership cannot be ignored. Team recruitment, team management, team culture, and communication are all vital aspects of leading a team. Team members will feel more secure and serve more effectively when they know what to expect and how they fit into the team. Establishing the rhythms of how your team functions creates unity and consistency when you meet. If you do not establish the practical matters as a leader, they will occur naturally—however, the outcomes may not be what you want. A strong leader sets the tone for the team through clear communication, specific expectations, and excellent organization. The way your team functions week to week determines how effective you will be. We want to be effective as intercessors. The spiritual health of the church depends on it. The practical matters of leadership support and empower what your team does and whether or not it is successful.

10

SUCCESSION PLANNING

WHEN YOU ARE IN A LEADERSHIP POSITION, ONE OF THE LAST things you normally think about is making yourself redundant. For most of us, it takes a lot of work and patience to reach a position of leadership, and once you have obtained it, you generally do not want to consider the possibility of relinquishing it. We like to be in control and tend not to let go of power voluntarily. Most of us like the feeling of calling the shots. Whether in a secular role in our career or a role in ministry, we like to be the one making the decisions.

There is nothing wrong with authority and leadership, but if we are to lead like Jesus, we must be continually looking to raise up and empower those around us. Although this might seem counterproductive to maintaining your position, developing emerging leaders raises your leadership up concurrently with those following you. Jesus was an incredible leader, and His legacy continues thousands of years later as evidenced by the spread of Christianity across the world. He invested in His disciples, who in turn invested in others, which enabled the gospel to spread from a few Jewish men and women to millions of believers throughout history.

Regardless of the group you are leading, succession planning should be a priority. Who are the people you are investing in personally? Who are the individuals you have recognized who have the potential to be the leaders of tomorrow? We must remember that we will not be in the same position forever. Things change. We move on. May I dare say it, we will die! It is irresponsible for a leader to ignore planning for the future. Leading an intercessory prayer team requires us to think ahead to grow the ministry and prepare it for the time when we are no longer there. If something changes, you do not want your church to be left without a competent intercessory prayer team able to carry on without you. I think it is the pinnacle of pride to think that we are the only ones who can lead our team. So, ask yourself, "If I was unable to continue leading my team tomorrow, what would happen?" You may be dismayed at the answer to this question if you have not been intentionally building leaders from those who follow you.

It breaks my heart to talk to other pastors whose churches have refused to consider the future and are now ageing in their community. They have lost their relevance, which consequently has minimized their ability to reach the people in their area. When the same people do the same things indefinitely without a thought of building others up around them, there comes a point where ministry will hit a ceiling, unable to go further. Whether it is a lack of leadership on the part of the pastors or the stubbornness of the congregation to change, there are many churches that will not exist in another ten to twenty years because everyone will either be too old to contribute or dead. Unfortunately, those are the cold, hard realities some churches are facing. If we are unwilling to delegate responsibility to others to help them grow as leaders, we will limit the ministry and set up a dynamic where a handful of people are in charge and no one else will be included. The few will do most of the work while others sit idle. New ideas and initiatives will be missed because there are no opportunities for emerging leaders to contribute, gain experience, or share ideas. Those in leadership roles may be comfortable there, but the church will not grow and flourish without the intentional development of the next generation of leaders.

I had about three years to prepare my ministry teams for my absence in advance of my extended family trip around Australia in 2020. While I was away, I spent time praying and discussing my future with my wife. When I left for this extended trip, I had every intention of returning to my pastoral role at the church. God had other plans. After about five months, I felt more and more confident that God was inviting me to begin a new journey in ministry. This book is one of the first steps in that new journey. When I returned to Brisbane, I knew it was time to make a difficult and scary decision to resign from the church I had been serving for fourteen years. I was comfortable in my role and loved serving alongside my volunteer teams, so the move was a leap of faith, but I knew I would regret not taking the risk.

I was fortunate to have the time and foresight to prepare my teams to function without me. My decision to resign would have been even more stressful had I not had confidence that the ministries could continue with new leadership. Not only have they continued, but they have also thrived in certain areas. The ease of this leadership transition occurred because I had competent second and third-tier leaders in place before I left. They were familiar with handling the varied responsibilities of leadership. The burden of responsibility can be a positive experience when there is support behind it, which is why I intentionally included my second and third-tier leaders in decision-making and gave them a large degree of responsibility and authority before I took leave. I gave them opportunities to plan and strategize with me. We discussed problematic issues, and they worked with me to develop healthy resolutions. I gave them responsibility to make decisions and implement programs. These emerging leaders knew they could fail while their leadership skills were developing because I was there to back them up, which is why I wanted them to begin stepping into leadership roles well before I became absent.

When I was no longer there to lean on, they were empowered and experienced to make decisions, and had the respect of the rest of the team to follow their leadership. They also knew the culture that had been established and were able to step into leading without the normal obstacles that a raw, fresh leader must navigate.

Let Someone Else Drive

I understand that many churches are not resource rich with capable and enthusiastic volunteers. This makes succession planning all the more necessary and vital. At first glance, you may not be able to identify possible candidates for leadership development. I urge you to pray that God will send someone your way. Lack of viable candidates is one problem, but a leader who is unwilling to raise up others around them is even more problematic. I understand that serving and leading can become personal when you have invested time, money, talent, and even your heart in the ministry. It can be difficult to let go of the steering wheel and let someone else drive, but it is essential if the ministry is to survive in the long term. In the short term, investing in new leaders can help the ministry thrive. This is true whether you are leading intercessors or any other ministry of your church.

Raising up new leaders also keeps you from doing too

much individually, which guards against burnout and exhaustion. The church is meant to function as a body with many parts operating to accomplish many tasks. If we neglect to include a part of the body, the whole organism suffers for it (1 Cor. 12:27). As pastors or voluntary ministry leaders, we must be willing to let go of some of our authority so those around us can grow. If we do not, we will be stagnating and limiting the ministry in the future.

The Model of Jesus

Jesus was a great leader. Although He was more than capable of doing the ministry Himself, He often gave His disciples responsibility even though they were not always ready for it. He let them fail and then lovingly taught them how to keep going and growing. Remember, His disciples came from many diverse backgrounds. They were not the best and brightest when it came to religious aptitude. If they were, they would have probably been Pharisees. Instead, they were fishermen, tax collectors, and ordinary men and women. They each carried their own flaws, just like the volunteers at your church. Jesus was able to see beyond their rough exteriors to recognize their potential. He saw their hearts because He sees us differently than we see each other (1 Sam. 16:7). Yes, they made mistakes continually. Yes, they could be frustrating at times, but they were committed, and Jesus used them to build His church and spread the gospel to the world.

God is not looking for perfect people, and neither should we. Like the loaves and fishes, God can multiply whatever we bring so that it is more than sufficient for the need (Matt. 14:13-21).

Servant Leadership

If there is one aspect of Jesus' leadership that we should emulate, it is His servant's heart. He was a servant leader, and I believe that is the model of leadership we should demonstrate as leaders within the church. This type of leadership naturally develops emerging leaders because the main leader puts his or her followers before themselves. Servant leaders are not concerned with being in charge or being seen as successful. Servant leaders focus on investing in their followers so they attain their full potential and success. If they win, the leader wins. At the Last Supper, Jesus explained His approach to leadership as He talked with His disciples over their Passover meal.

> *A dispute also arose among them as to which of them was considered to be greatest. Jesus said to them, "The kings of the Gentiles lord it over them; and those who exercise authority over them call themselves Benefactors. But you are not to be like that. Instead, the greatest among you should be like the youngest, and the*

one who rules like the one who serves. For who is greater, the one who is at the table or the one who serves? Is it not the one who is at the table? But I am among you as one who serves. You are those who have stood by me in my trials. And I confer on you a kingdom, just as my Father conferred one on me, so that you may eat and drink at my table in my kingdom and sit on thrones, judging the twelve tribes of Israel.

— LUKE 22:24-30

In another powerful passage from this same night, Jesus humbled Himself and modeled servant leadership as He washed the disciples' feet. In Jewish culture, the task of washing feet was often reserved for the lowliest of servants. Anyone of any prominence would never lower themselves to perform this job. Yet, Jesus lovingly washed the feet of His disciples to teach them that a servant heart is preferred over prestige or position. Jesus knew who He was and was not afraid to humble Himself to serve His disciples. By demonstrating humility, Jesus did not lose His identity or become less worthy. He was not worried about losing His position because His relationship with God and the disciples was intimate and strong. When you are developing emerging leaders, you must demonstrate this kind of selfless love as well.

Jesus' love for each of His disciples was His motivation to perform this humble task.

> *It was just before the Passover Festival. Jesus knew that the hour had come for him to leave this world and go to the Father. Having loved his own who were in the world, he loved them to the end. The evening meal was in progress, and the devil had already prompted Judas, the son of Simon Iscariot, to betray Jesus. Jesus knew that the Father had put all things under his power, and that he had come from God and was returning to God; so, he got up from the meal, took off his outer clothing, and wrapped a towel around his waist. After that, he poured water into a basin and began to wash his disciples' feet, drying them with the towel that was wrapped around him.*
>
> — JOHN 13:1-5

As Jesus began to wash the disciples' feet, Peter spoke without thinking. He emotionally protested because he knew this was culturally inappropriate and did not want to embarrass or abuse Jesus, His Lord. Peter did not understand the significance of this act until Jesus explained it to him.

He came to Simon Peter, who said to him, "Lord, are you going to wash my feet?" Jesus replied, "You do not realize now what I am doing, but later you will understand." "No," said Peter, "you shall never wash my feet." Jesus answered, "Unless I wash you, you have no part with me." "Then, Lord," Simon Peter replied, "not just my feet but my hands and my head as well!"

— JOHN 13:6-9

Jesus used this experience to teach His disciples how they should lead. This was one of the last nights that He would spend with them. Knowing that His time was near to be crucified, Jesus was instilling in His disciples the most important things for them to remember and apply in the future. It is interesting to note that serving one another is the key message.

When he had finished washing their feet, he put on his clothes and returned to his place. "Do you understand what I have done for you?" he asked them. "You call me 'Teacher' and 'Lord,' and rightly so, for that is what I am. Now that I, your Lord and Teacher, have washed your feet, you also should wash one another's feet. I have set you an example that you should do as I have done for you. Very truly I tell you, no servant is greater than his master, nor is a messenger greater than the one who sent him. Now that you know these things, you will be blessed if you do them.

— JOHN 13:12-17

The point that Jesus made by washing the disciples' feet is a point that we should take to heart as we invest in the next generation of leaders. We must lead by lifting up those around us by earnestly serving them so they may reach their full potential. We cannot lead from a position of pride, expecting others to serve our own ambitions. When we put others first, we will reap the blessings of God.

A Christian leader should view themselves as a servant. This may mean that we make ourselves redundant eventually, which is not a negative outcome. In fact, this is the greatest success as a Christian leader. We must humble ourselves so others may be promoted. We cannot worry about trivial things such as titles and positions. Jesus knew who He was and was willing to serve and raise up others for the benefit of the kingdom. Like Jesus, we cannot let our position or title define our identity or our actions. Jesus was still Lord to the disciples after He washed their feet. Our value is found in our relationship with God, not what we do for Him.

That was one of the mistakes the Pharisees made. They thought their righteousness, justification, and value were determined by how well they followed the numerous Jewish laws and rules. This did not create humble, loving servants. Instead, it created prideful, selfish men who craved power and prestige. Jesus modeled servanthood as the greatest form of leadership. We best serve our emerging leaders when we give them opportunities to lead and take on leadership responsibilities with our support. We are there to train and equip them to succeed in life and ministry. Jesus demonstrated this pattern throughout His time on earth.

Sending Out the Disciples

Jesus would regularly send out His disciples to do ministry in the neighboring towns, investing in the twelve by living and ministering with them for three years. He answered their questions and taught them how to live out their faith and minister to the needs of others. He also invested in the larger circle of disciples who were following Him. The following passages demonstrate how Jesus would empower and release His disciples to do ministry. He gave them specific instructions that set up specific expectations. At times the results were mixed, but more often than not, the disciples would return with testimonies of victory over the enemy and lives being transformed by the gospel.

When Jesus had called the Twelve together, he gave them power and authority to drive out all demons and to cure diseases, and he sent them out to proclaim the kingdom of God and to heal the sick. He told them: "Take nothing for the journey—no staff, no bag, no bread, no money, no extra shirt. Whatever house you enter, stay there until you leave that town. If people do not welcome you, leave their town and shake the dust off your feet as a testimony against them." So, they set out and went from village to village, proclaiming the good news and healing people everywhere.

— LUKE 9:1-6

After this the Lord appointed seventy-two others and sent them two by two ahead of him to every town and place where he was about to go. He told them, "The harvest is plentiful, but the workers are few. Ask the Lord of the harvest, therefore, to send out workers into his harvest field. Go! I am sending you out like lambs among wolves. Do not take a purse or bag or sandals; and do not greet anyone on the road. When you enter a house, first say, 'Peace to this house.' If someone who promotes peace is there, your peace will rest on them; if not, it will return to you. Stay there, eating and drinking whatever they give you, for the worker deserves his wages. Do not move around from house to house. When you enter a town and are welcomed, eat what is offered to you. Heal the sick who are there and tell them, 'The kingdom of God has come near to you.' But when you enter a town and are not welcomed, go into its streets and say, 'Even the dust of your town we wipe from our feet as a warning to you. Yet be sure of this: The kingdom of God has come near.'"

— LUKE 10:1-11

Specific Instructions and Expectations are Vital

In both passages from Luke 9 and 10, Jesus gave specific instructions to His disciples in how they were to go about ministering in the towns. Some of the things He told them to do seem odd, but have a purpose in preparing them for when He would no longer be there to lead them. For instance, He told His disciples not to take any money or provisions for their journey. Instead, they were to find food, shelter, and support from those in the town who accepted them. I believe this was to teach them to be reliant on God and to learn to trust that He would meet their needs as they ministered. These would be valuable traits once Jesus had been crucified and returned to the Father. The disciples had to be reliant on God despite their circumstances and resources.

Some instructions were for their safety, as Jesus told the disciples not to greet anyone on the road because He knew that thieves would often use the isolated and lonely stretches of roads to attack their victims. He also told them what to say and do if they were rejected by a house or town. In all these instances, Jesus was clear about what the disciples were to do and how they were to act.

When you are mentoring an emerging leader, it is important that your instructions and expectations are specific and clear. Giving someone responsibility without details and expectations for the outcome leaves them in a position that is vulnerable to failure. Jesus expected that the outcome of these trips would be that the sick would be healed, the demonized set free, and the good news proclaimed. This is what happened. *"The seventy-two returned with joy and said, 'Lord, even the demons submit to us in your name'"* (Luke 10:17). Notice that the outcome met the expectation. The disciples had previously seen Jesus model how to heal the sick and cast out demons as they traveled with Him.

Next, He gave them a chance to experience the Holy Spirit working through them to do the same. He foresaw some of the obstacles that they would face and instructed them in how to deal with things like rejection or lack of resources. We should do the same when we are raising up new leaders in our ministry. If we are not specific with our instructions and expectations, we do not have a standard to measure the new leaders by, and it becomes difficult to give constructive feedback or encouragement to help emerging leaders to continue to grow.

Paul's Spiritual Sons

The Apostle Paul was also a good example of how to raise up new leaders. At various times during his ministry, Paul brought emerging leaders with him on his journeys or assigned younger disciples to the churches that he had founded, encouraging these men and including them in the work he was doing in the churches he had planted. Paul knew that he would not be able to maintain all the churches he founded without emerging leaders in place. He was often in jail or isolated in some way, which prevented him from visiting all the churches he had planted. This also prevented Paul from directly resolving the conflicts that arose or ensuring that the gospel was preached accurately. These types of circumstances led Paul to set up emerging leaders in these churches to lead in his absence.

Timothy is one example of an emerging leader who was given significant responsibilities by Paul. In 1 Timothy 1:2, Paul calls Timothy *"my true son in the faith."* Paul and Timothy had cultivated a strong and supportive relationship with one another, and Paul saw Timothy as someone who reflected his leadership and beliefs. Paul had founded the church in Ephesus where Timothy was serving, but he trusted Timothy to act on his behalf to enforce discipline against the elders who were taking the church in a wrong direction. Paul also relied on Timothy to continue to lead the church toward Christ while he was absent. Paul writes to Timothy, *"Although I hope to come to you soon, I am writing you these instructions so that, if I am delayed, you will know how people ought to conduct themselves in God's household, which is the church of the living God, the pillar and foundation of the truth"* (1 Tim. 3:14-15). This a great responsibility for a young man, but Paul fully trusted Timothy because he had spent time with him teaching and training him to lead the church. Paul continued to encourage and build Timothy up so he would remain faithful to the message and mission of Jesus.

Timothy, my son, I am giving you this command in keeping with the prophecies once made about you, so that by recalling them you may fight the battle well, holding on to faith and a good conscience, which some have rejected and so have suffered shipwreck with regard to the faith. Among them are Hymenaeus and Alexander, whom I have handed over to Satan to be taught not to blaspheme.

— 1 TIMOTHY 1:18-20

Consistent Encouragement

At the end of Paul's ministry, when he was imprisoned and anticipating his imminent death, he wrote once again to Timothy to pass the baton of leadership. Even at the end, Paul was still encouraging and building Timothy up. Like Jesus, Paul specifically instructs Timothy, *"Do your best to present yourself to God as one approved, a worker who does not need to be ashamed and who correctly handles the word of truth"* (2 Tim. 2:15). Paul reminded Timothy to remember the things that he had taught him. *"What you heard from me, keep as the pattern of sound teaching, with faith and love in Christ Jesus. Guard the good deposit that was entrusted to you—guard it with the help of the Holy Spirit who lives in us"* (2 Tim. 1:13-14).

Much of what Paul said to Timothy reflects the values and characteristics we see in Paul's personal ministry. Primarily, Paul encouraged Timothy to hold on to the gospel of Jesus Christ and to always keep Jesus the focal point of ministry. Everything Paul believed in and preached is centered on Jesus, His sacrifice on the cross, His resurrection, and the implications of believing in Him. Paul poured his life into Timothy and developed him as a leader to continue to instruct others in a similar way, knowing he could depend on Timothy to lead the church even though Paul was imprisoned many miles away.

As you continue to read the book of 2 Timothy, Paul seems to be giving Timothy some final instructions as he anticipates his death. The love, respect, and camaraderie between Timothy and Paul is evident.

You, however, know all about my teaching, my way of life, my purpose, faith, patience, love, endurance, persecutions, sufferings—what kinds of things happened to me in Antioch, Iconium and Lystra, the persecutions I endured. Yet the Lord rescued me from all of them.

But as for you, continue in what you have learned and have become convinced of, because you know those from whom you learned it and how from infancy you have known the Holy Scriptures, which are able to make you wise for salvation through faith in Christ Jesus.

— 2 TIMOTHY 3:10-11, 14-15

Timothy transitioned from a young, enthusiastic disciple to a valuable, trusted leader in the church because Paul had invested the time and training required to develop him into a powerful leader and minister of the gospel. As a result, Timothy was able to carry the characteristics and culture that Paul had established and was able to reproduce himself by training others as he had been trained and mentored by Paul. In this way, whether Paul was present or absent, the gospel could continue to be faithfully preached and established in the early church. As gentiles, we are a living legacy of Paul's ministry many, many years later.

Invest in Multiple Leaders

Timothy is most likely the best example of Paul's efforts to develop emerging leaders. However, he was not the only one. In Paul's closing statements of 2 Timothy, we get a glimpse of the many young men Paul was developing.

> *Do your best to come to me quickly, for Demas, because he loved this world, has deserted me and has gone to Thessalonica. Crescens has gone to Galatia, and Titus to Dalmatia. Only Luke is with me. Get Mark and bring him with you, because he is helpful to me in my ministry. I sent Tychicus to Ephesus. When you come, bring the cloak that I left with Carpus at Troas, and my scrolls, especially the parchments.*
>
> — 2 TIMOTHY 4:9-13

In this passage, Paul mentions multiple disciples who were serving with him. Demas, Crescens, Titus, Luke, Mark, and Tychicus were all ministering and growing under Paul's leadership. I am sure there were others who are not mentioned in this passage. Paul had sent several of them out to continue to support the churches in Ephesus, Thessalonica, Galatia, and Dalmatia. However, not all of them became church leaders. Demas seems to have abandoned Paul because he loved the world more than he loved the gospel. When we are developing emerging leaders, we must remember that not all of them will be successful. We cannot get discouraged by the ones who say it is too hard or get distracted by other opportunities.

Do Not Get Discouraged

When I was serving as the young adult pastor at Riverlife, I made multiple attempts to develop emerging leaders. Regretfully, I was unsuccessful in many cases. I lost leaders to other ministries, to apathy, and to simple flakiness. There were people who expressed a desire to lead, but were not willing to follow through with the effort required to fulfill their responsibilities and were not committed to the ministry. Many times, I felt discouraged because I was the one who had to fill in the gaps they left behind. This put stress on me as the pastor because I was responsible for the ministry to continue despite my plans changing. I made mistakes in choosing who I invested in. Instead of waiting to see who was consistently committed and faithful, I gave responsibility to the first person who put their hand up to lead.

Thankfully, I learned from these failures, which meant

that I was more successful at developing leaders later in my ministry. I learned to choose leaders who were already demonstrating leadership before being given official responsibility, which turned out to be a much more successful model. This does not mean that everyone you invest in will become a leader. Paul humbly admits that some of his emerging leaders abandoned him when he needed them most. This may happen to you too. Do not let discouragement distract you from the calling God has placed on your life. You must press forward even when things do not turn out the way you had hoped. God will bless your faithfulness.

As leaders in the church, whether we are in a paid pastoral role or serving as a volunteer leader, we must invest in the emerging leaders who are following us. Succession planning is a priority. It takes time and intentionality, but you will reap the benefits of your efforts for years to come if you do not give up. Jesus modeled how to develop leaders by giving specific instructions and expectations from the beginning. He included them in His work so they could gain experience and grow as leaders themselves. Jesus gave His disciples the freedom to fail, learn from the failure, and return better for it. He lovingly prepared His disciples to lead the church once He was no longer walking the earth. We cannot get discouraged by setbacks. Instead, we must continue to seek out and develop emerging leaders so they can take our place eventually. Most leaders are measured by the success of their organization or group. The people who make that success happen are the ones following the leader. We all succeed when we invest in the tiers of emerging leaders following us. As their ceiling rises, so does ours.

As you commit yourself to lead in a manner worthy of Christ, take time to return often to embrace the most excellent words of scripture, such as those the Apostle Paul wrote to the church in Ephesus.

For this reason I kneel before the Father, from whom every family in heaven and on earth derives its name. I pray that out of his glorious riches he may strengthen you with power through his Spirit in your inner being, so that Christ may dwell in your hearts through faith. And I pray that you, being rooted and established in love, may have power, together with all the Lord's holy people, to grasp how wide and long and high and deep is the love of Christ, and to know this love that surpasses knowledge—that you may be filled to the measure of all the fullness of God. Now to him who is able to do immeasurably more than all we ask or imagine, according to his power that is at work within us, to him be glory in the church and in Christ Jesus throughout all generations, for ever and ever! Amen.

— EPHESIANS 3:14-21

11

FINAL THOUGHTS

The principles and practicalities that I have shared in this book have often come through finding ways to overcome the obstacles blocking my goals and responsibilities as a pastor. By God's grace, He has lovingly and patiently revealed how to pray with others to see His will done. He is the source of all wisdom and understanding. I am thankful for what I have received and excited to have shared it with you.

I believe in the power of prayer. It is a weapon that God has given to connect us to His power and release His will in our world. I am perpetually amazed at how the simple act of speaking (or even thinking) words can significantly change dire situations into blessings.

Prayer is more than a weapon to tear down strongholds—it is a tremendous gift! When we use this gift in service to others through intercession, both the intercessor and the recipient are blessed. When we intercede, we have access to God's power, grace, hope, healing, blessings, and peace. We need these things in abundance as we live as believers, and God generously responds to us when we pray.

Every church would benefit from the development of an intercessory prayer team. I cannot emphasize too strongly the importance of being covered in prayer as a church ministers to its community. The enemy does not want to see your church prosper. He is constantly working to undermine the message of the gospel. Intercession confronts the enemy where he is working and removes his ability to cause disruption or disunity within the church.

Every church must navigate challenges and adversity. Without intercessors, your church is much more vulnerable to the attacks of the enemy. Wouldn't it be better to face our problems with God's insight, wisdom, and power than to try to solve them on our own? This is where a group of mature, faithful intercessors can make all the difference.

If you are a pastor or ministry leader, please consider developing an intercessory prayer team for your church or ministry. The benefit far outweighs the effort. I am confident that you will see a change in the spiritual atmosphere of your church once a dedicated group of people start praying on a consistent basis. Not only will the spiritual atmosphere change, but there will be measurable fruit in the lives of your attendees.

If there was one key message I would like for you to take

away from reading this book, it would be to prioritize prayer. We often save prayer as our last option. I'm encouraging you to pray first. I guarantee you will put in less effort and see greater results if you start by praying.

If you do not have enough people to develop a full team of intercessors, start with two or three. Jesus will be with you as you pray! Start small and trust that God will build the team in time. If you apply the principles found in this book, you can quickly develop an intercessory prayer team that is effective and valuable.

When we intentionally prioritize prayer, it not only changes our circumstances, it changes us. Prayer brings us into God's presence where we can commune with Him. We experience His love and renew our faith when we pray. Time in God's presence is always transformative.

As you finish reading this book, I pray you experience a new passion for prayer. I hope you will apply these principles and see God do incredible things through your church. May you draw closer to God's heart so you can understand His will and partner with His ways. I pray your church becomes a beacon of light in your community that will draw many to a saving knowledge of Jesus Christ.

Want more?

Download a FREE 7-day devotional on prayer to help kick start your new prayer life and put the things you've learned into practice.

VISIT: www.kingfisherministries.com

You'll also get access to my other resources and I'll keep you up to date on new releases, training programs and more.

If you enjoyed "Armed" or learned something new through reading it, please leave a review where you bought it. Reviews help authors to find other readers who could benefit from reading their books. Every review is much appreciated.

ABOUT THE AUTHOR

Eric M. Whitley is the founder of *Kingfisher Ministries* in Brisbane, Australia. *Kingfisher Ministries* was established to train and equip churches around the world to pray with power, minister with excellence, and release God's will over the communities they serve. With over 25 years of pastoral experience in the United States and Australia, Eric shares unique and insightful perspectives to pastoral ministry. *Armed* is his first book.

www.ingramcontent.com/pod-product-compliance
Lightning Source LLC
Chambersburg PA
CBHW071607080526
44588CB00010B/1051